The Hudson River Almanac
Volume VI, 1999-2000

Governor George E. Pataki, NYS DEC Commissioner John P. Cahill, and DEC biologist, Pete Nye with bald eagle

Hudson River Estuary Program
NYS Department of Environmental Conservation
George E. Pataki, Governor
John P. Cahill, Commissioner

Hudson River Estuary

Purple Mountain Press
Fleischmanns, New York

The Hudson River Almanac: Vol. VI, 1999-2000

First Edition

Published by Purple Mountain Press, Ltd.
1060 Main Street, PO Box 309
Fleischmanns, New York 12430-0378
845-254-4062, 845-254-4476 (fax)
1-800-325-2665

Waterlily   by Esther Kiviat

For further information on the Hudson River Almanac Project, contact:

The Hudson River Estuary Program
NYS Department of Environmental Conservation
21 South Putt Corners Road
New Paltz, New York 12561
845-256-3016, 845-255-3649 (fax)

Manufactured in the United States of America
Printed with soy-based ink on acid-free, recycled paper.

Table of Contents

Acknowledgments

The Hudson River Almanac would like to acknowledge and thank the following for their partnership and enthusiasm: The Hudson River Foundation for Science and Environmental Research, The Greenway Conservancy for the Hudson River Valley, Inc., The Hudson River Improvement Fund, New England Interstate Water Pollution Control Commission, the Hudson River Almanac Scientific Advisory Committee, and the hundreds of observers and contributors.

Cover photograph by Esther Kiviat. Many others throughout this volume are from her book, *Changing Tides: Tivoli Bays,* published by Purple Mountain Press.

Hudson River Almanac Staff

Frances Dunwell   Project Manager
Tom Lake   Editor/Field Coordinator
Bethia Waterman   Copy Editor/Designer
Christopher Lake   Editorial Assistant

Almanac Web Site

http://www.dec.state.ny.us/website/hudson/alm/html

STATE OF NEW YORK

GEORGE E. PATAKI
GOVERNOR

Dear New Yorkers:

I am pleased to announce the availability of Volume VI of the *Hudson River Almanac*. The *Almanac*, a project of New York State Department of Environmental Conservation's Hudson River Estuary Program, is an annual natural history journal that records events throughout the year in the Hudson River Valley. It is a product of a partnership between citizen volunteers and state government.

The *Almanac* began six years ago with the goal of inspiring New Yorkers to a better appreciation of one of our State's greatest natural resources. The first six volumes have included the contributions of more than 2000 participants of all ages, from elementary school students to scientists to philosophers. Each participant has had a unique perspective to share and their stories have helped change the way we look at our environment and affirmed for us the magic and majesty of the Hudson River. We all are perpetual students, and like a good teacher, the River requires that we summon the curiosity to ask questions, the desire to know the answers, and the patience to seek them out.

Volume VI documents the 12 months from the vernal equinox of 1999 to the vernal equinox of 2000. It tells a story of changing seasons, of droughts and storms, of today and of a time, long ago, when people first walked along the River's shores.

The Spring of 1999 produced five bald eaglets on the River, doubling our total since 1997. This is an ongoing success story of habitat protection and stewardship for which we can all be proud. Summer brought with it the most extreme drought in 105 years, setting daily records for high temperatures during July and setting ablaze Dunderberg Mountain in the Hudson Highlands for several weeks in August. Relief came in September in the form of tropical storm Floyd. Born of a hurricane, Floyd swept across the Adirondack's High Peaks with torrential rains, floods, and high winds. In mid-winter the Hudson Valley went into a deep freeze, icing over many of the upland wintering areas for bald eagles, such as New York City's reservoirs in the Catskill Mountains. By February, the relatively open water of the lower Hudson had become a refuge. Observers there spotted as many as 60 eagles in one day on ice floes and perched along the River. These extremes in weather provided the backdrop for the observations that defined the past year in the life of the Hudson River.

Whether it's catching tidewater striped bass in Spring, fly fishing cool mountain waters in Summer, hiking to Lake Tear in Fall, or watching a pair of bald eagles drift down the river on an ice floe in winter, our 320 miles of Hudson River truly has something for everyone to enjoy. The *Almanac* helps us connect with these activities by allowing us to share our excitement and discoveries in its pages. I encourage you to take the opportunity to document your own experiences on the Hudson, and by doing so, enrich our knowledge of the River's unique natural history.

Very truly yours,

George E. Pataki

Marsh Marigolds   by Esther Kiviat

Spring

March 1999

The continents themselves dissolve and pass to the sea,
in grain after grain of eroded land.
So the rains that rose from it return again in rivers.
Rachel Carson, *The Sea Around Us*

Vernal Equinox

3/20 Ice Meadows, HRM 245: In early morning on the first day of spring, the Ice Meadows had a glacial look about it. Along the river we found two rectangular holes drilled into the trunk of a tall white pine, about eight inches off the ground—pileated woodpeckers feasting on carpenter ants. The holes, one over the other, were 4-inches-wide, 13" high, and 7 inches deep. We headed out onto the river, traversing an ice field, crevasses yawning beneath our footsteps, to reach the edge of flowing water. We found ourselves atop twenty-foot vertical walls of ice. At the end of the river, 250 miles south, it was 70°F and spring; here, it was still decidedly winter. *Tom Lake, Christopher Letts*

Tahawus, HRM 309: As we walked along the main road in the ghost town of Tahawus, we heard whispers. It turned out to be the wind coming through the red spruce. At least that's what we told ourselves. Scores of evening grosbeaks flitted from tree limb to tree limb, shaking newly fallen snow off the boughs of balsam. Red squirrels raced about like the frenetic little critters they are. We saw some tracks in the new snow and, after some deliberation, decided they were bobcat. At least one, maybe two, had sauntered down the middle of this logging road. Ravens spoke to us at every turn, and where the sun had melted the snow, gritty crossbills pecked at the dirt left by the sander. It was a perfect day for an equinox, a perfect place to begin anew. *Tom Lake, Christopher Letts*

A **raven** can be distinguished from a crow, in addition to its larger size and its call (*croak* rather than *caw*), by its wedge-shaped tail, best seen in flight.

Calamity Brook, HRM 311: The Hudson's headwaters ran cold and clear between banks of near waist-deep snow. Red-breasted nuthatches called from every quarter. Winter held its grip on the High Peaks and it was difficult to picture spring anywhere but in our hearts. *Tom Lake, Christopher Letts*

3/21 Lake Colden, HRM 311: I skied up the Calamity Brook Trail from Tahawus, the Upper Works trailhead, and across Lake Colden to Avalanche Lake on the first day of the year. It was sunny and 36°F with a deep and soft, medium-fast snow pack. I stopped at the hanging wood plank way under the sheer cliffs of Avalanche Mountain as the wind was howling off Algonquin Peak (5114') and Mount Colden (4714') which flank this most spectacular source water of the Hudson River. Storm clouds were moving in from the southwest. Downward from this 2863' High Peaks frozen lake to Newcomb and further, past North Creek, the Ice Meadows, and Glens Falls, the river takes a final big bend and heads south to New York City still more than 200 miles away. They'll have rain downriver while this gorged lake will fill with snow again tonight. *Doug Reed*

1

The Whispering Watershed
Slowly water trickles down,
Deep below the ground.
You'll never see or hear it,
Even if you're near it.
Eventually it will run out,
Deep into the river's mouth.
It brings with it different bugs,
mayflies, stone flies, even slugs.
It has been on a wonderful journey,
Searching for the open river's beauty.
Now the search is over,
But without knowing,
More water is trickling down.
Dan Sunderlin, New Windsor School, NY

Town of Durham, HRM 124: I was passing an aspen that had the top half broken off in a windstorm. A cavity had been excavated, about twelve feet up the tree, several years ago, and I noticed a feather caught on the entrance. I gave the tree a couple kicks and a saw-whet owl popped its head out. I hear them regularly in late February and March with their monotonous, whistled call, but this was the first time I had found a nest. *Larry Biegel*

3/23 Esopus, HRM 87: The first phoebe was back and singing. Many more would arrive over the next few days. *Bill Drakert*

Croton River, HRM 34: What a sweet morning. I was at the riverbank well before daybreak. At 6:15 AM, as the light grew, several tree swallows were skimming the bay by the railroad bridge. Where there were a half dozen yesterday, now there were more than a hundred. As the sun crested the treeline I looked up to see more than a hundred of them roosting in a stubby hawthorn. They were slowly waking up, perched toward the rising sun, the first rays glinting off their shiny white breasts. *Christopher Letts*

3/24 Esopus, HRM 87: A real sign of spring: We heard peepers tonight—faint but surely there. *Bill Drakert*

Calamity Brook   by Tom Lake

Ellis Island, New York Harbor: While ascending the third floor staircase of the abandoned and dilapidated New Hospital Extension Building *(ca.* 1908) on Island 2, I found myself 15' from a fledgling barn owl perched atop a rusty newel post. The floor behind it was littered with pellets, dead pigeons, and a dead Norway rat. Though known for decades to be indigenous here, this was the first verified nesting site. The unique aspect of this sighting was its earliness. Normally, breeding begins in March but the mild winter allowed breeding to begin as early as January. *Jim Elkin, Dave McCutcheon*

Breezy Point, New York Bight: One of the harbingers of spring for beach strollers, birders, and naturalists at Breezy Point—the eastern gateway to the Hudson River estuary—is the return of the piping plover. These wading birds are protected by the Federal Endangered Species Act. Their numbers have declined in recent years due to beach disturbance, so

2

known nesting areas are protected during the breeding season. *Dave Taft*

Piping plover first observed

<u>1999</u>	<u>1998</u>	<u>1997</u>	<u>1996</u>	<u>1995</u>	<u>1994</u>
3/25	3/24	3/20	3/15	3/16	3/11

Yonkers, HRM 18: We were not used to having our beach seine come in from a haul with only a single fish in it. On this occasion, however, we were not complaining. Our "catch" was a juvenile spotted hake (75 mm). Salinity was 4.0 ppt; water temperature was 42°F. *David Rosenfeld* (See Vol.IV:57 for another spotted hake record.)

Spotted hake are a member of the codfish family and are rather uncommon visitors to the Hudson River. They are fall marine water spawners. This individual may have been from last autumn's crop that moved into the brackish lower river, a nursery area, seeking forage and shelter from predation.

3/26 Esopus, HRM 87: Our first coltsfoot was out, a bit late this year. *Bill Drakert*

Croton Point, HRM 34.5: The landfill looked like a train station at rush hour; birds, new arrivals from wintering range, were flying everywhere at once. Four American kestrels were in view. A male and a female were perched on poles and two others were hovering into the northwest wind 15' over the ground, looking for forage. A pair of northern harriers were dipping and rising over the hillside, on the hunt. Perched on another pole, looking quite regal, was an immature red-shouldered hawk. Song sparrows cautiously flitted around the base of the hill—better to stay inconspicuous than become dinner. As if to prove that point, a crow flew past carrying a sparrow in its beak. *Bob Keyes, Christopher Letts, Tom Lake*

3/27 Croton Point, HRM 35: Seventy-five students, parents, and teachers from *Post Road School*, White Plains, swarmed onto the bathing beach with rakes and trash bags, and went to work with a will. After two hours an entire half year's worth of flotsam, jetsam, and river debris was piled above the high tide line. It seemed no

log or stump was capable of resisting the energy and teamwork of the group. Prize finds: a dry and odorless carcass of a mute swan, half a dozen fine examples of beaver sticks, and several pairs of sunglasses. In all, about ten dump truck loads of material. *Christopher Letts*

Wild turkeys   by Esther Kiviat

Beaver sticks are a feature of almost any walk along a beach on the Hudson. These gnawed pieces of poplar, maple, birch or other deciduous tree—the ends of which have a whittled taper—range in size from a few inches to more than four-feet-long. They are the product of a beaver meal. Having stripped off the leaves, tender twigs, even the bark, they are set adrift in ponds, streams and lakes, eventually finding their way down through the watershed to be washed up on a beach in tidewater. As *Christopher Letts* says, finding a beaver stick is like getting a postcard from an old friend.

Nyack, HRM 28: *Robert Gabrielson Jr.* set and picked his herring gillnet and caught the first two river herring of the year. He lost little time in turning one of the alewives into cut bait and soon landed a 42" striped bass.

3/29 Town of Wappinger, HRM 68: With the very mild winter we had I thought that the spring peepers would sing their song much earlier this year. Not so. The first ones I heard were tonight, which was a day later than last year. *Vince Francese*

3/30 Lattintown Creek, HRM 68.5: River herring were on their way from the sea and this tributary had a reputation as a good spawning stream for alewives. For the next two months, I would try to determine just how good it was by measuring the strength and productivity of its river herring. As I ambled down the trail to the creek at first light, I came upon a pair of wild turkeys. As they flew away across the water they sounded like 747s. No sooner had they left and a pair of wood ducks whistled past. My presence was not going unnoticed. Male red-winged blackbirds perched in the angular black willows and scolded me for intruding. (I will have to stop wearing my red sweatshirt. I'm sure they view me as the biggest alpha male they have ever seen.) In the creek a couple of muskrats kept watch from just below some research nets I had set earlier. I could see male white suckers with breeding tubercles moving up above the reach of tide to spawn. Using a dip net I caught a 19" male sucker replete with a dash of crimson along each lateral line—breeding colors. I released a 13" brown trout that would have been fair game on a rod and reel in just two days. Although I was sheltered in the lee of the surrounding high ground, I could hear the roar at the tree tops and out on the river gale force wind gusts to 40 mph were producing a blowout tide. *Tom Lake, Gregg Hogancamp*

River herring research was being conducted in the Hudson River, its tidal tributaries, and the Mohawk River to determine species distribution and productivity. Our two river herrings, alewives and bluebacks, arrive from the sea each spring, ascend the Hudson, and spawn. Most alewives spawn in tidal tributaries between Croton and Troy. Most bluebacks do not stop until they reach the Mohawk River. There is an occasional mix, such as in Rondout Creek, where both are found.

Croton Point, HRM 34: It was blowing half a gale out of the northwest but on the south side of the point the sun was warm. There was a contest going on between the bright blossoms of coltsfoot and the splendid yellow breasts of half a dozen meadowlarks. Before I could decide on a winner, a movement overhead caught my eye: a mature bald eagle hanging almost motionless in the wind several hundred feet above my head. *Christopher Letts*

3/31 Esopus Meadows, HRM 87: Canada geese were nesting with aggressive ganders guarding the nests under a Blue Moon. *Bill Drakert*

Blue moons, as you might expect, are uncommon. Only when a month has a second full moon, is it called blue. And that happens only once in a . . .

Croton Point, HRM 34.5: I know of no nicer place to dig a mess of dandelion greens than on the top of the landfill on this peninsula. This vernal pastime requires nice timing. If the flowers are in bloom, the greens will have turned too bitter to make good salad. The dandelions are so large on this hilltop, and so numerous, that I could dig all I needed in one spot. I picked a place with a good view of Croton Bay and went to work. The "mosquito fleet" (vessels smaller than 18') was out in full force in pursuit of striped bass. Flock after flock of high-flyer Canada geese disappeared into the northern sky. A juvenile bald eagle stood sentinel in a locust 150 yards away. *Christopher Letts*

"High-flyers" is a common description for migrating waterfowl, most often applied to geese. High-flyers, large undulating Vs or skeins of birds, can be well over a mile high. They are often heard long before they are seen, and even when seen appear only as a ragged line in the sky. The higher altitude is a more efficient way for them to travel between Canadian breeding grounds and wintering locations in the DelMarVa region.

April 1999

If, during April, one could render the river transparent and peer to the bottom of the channel,
the northward parade of anadromous fish would be staggering—one-hundred- to two-hundred-pound sturgeon
would ride the bottom below pods of ten- to sixty-pound striped bass and great shoals of shad.

John Waldman, *Heartbeats in the Muck*

4/1   Town of Esopus, HRM 88: There were snow geese as well as Canada geese feeding in the Hurley flats. In spring migration, snow geese tend to just fly over and do not land on the river, so it was nice to see them at eye level. *Fran Drakert, Bill Drakert*

4/2   Lattintown Creek, HRM 68.5: We caught a huge female alewife (321 mm) in our research nets tonight. A repeat spawner. Even though gillnets can be selective in the size of fish they catch, this alewife was 20% larger than the average. Since these ocean-run fish demonstrate some fidelity to their natal streams, today may have been this one's third springtime visit to this creek. *Tom Lake, Phyllis Lake*

Winding River Valley
Winding River, how do you flow?
Up hill, down hill, through rain, sleet and snow.
As you go through our town,
 our valley, our home,
everyone watches where you might roam.
Our lives are rushed, at such a fast pace,
when you flow by, your water we embrace.
The gentle breeze, the air in your hair,
from a ride along the river to anywhere.
Stephanie Rundle, Hendrick Hudson High School, Montrose, NY

4/3   Lattintown Creek, HRM 68.5: One of the joys of having a daily (and nightly) routine on the river is that you get to watch spring arrive. The black willows, hanging over the creek, were leafing out, white-throated sparrows were singing in chorus, and hundreds of migrating grackles and blackbirds filled the trees for an evening roost. In addition to river herring, our net caught a 20", ornately colored black and orange goldfish. *Tom Lake, Phyllis Lake*

Goldfish are not native to the Hudson River. They were inadvertently introduced through their use as bait, and also by being released by disillusioned parents ("My children promised to take care of the goldfish!").

4/4   Fort Miller, HRM 192.5: It was a crystal clear morning with light breezes and a heady sense of the wild and free and the ever flowing river. A group of twelve greater scaup floated and dove in mid-river, while a pair of lesser scaup stayed closer to shore. A lone pied-billed grebe kept to itself throughout the morning. I had hoped it had a mate nearby but there was no evidence of another. I was delighted to see a male bufflehead, known as the "spirit duck" among Canadian sportsmen. The sight which surprised me most was the appearance of six oldsquaw. This was the first time I had seen these ducks anywhere in the north country. The following day they were gone, continuing their long flight passage to coastal breeding grounds along the northern edges of our continent. *Jim Sotis*

4/5   Ellis Island/Statue of Liberty, New York Harbor: Today was the first that I noticed our magnolia and forsythia in full bloom. *Jim Elkin*

4/6   Wappinger Falls, HRM 67: The riverside was looking splendid in color as the forsythia and the magnolia was in bloom. *Tom Lake*

4/7   Croton Point, HRM 34.5: The early light was beautiful on top of the landfill. The strong south breeze carried the trilling of American toads up from the vernal ponds at the base of the hill. I was counting kestrels when I saw a large bird approaching from the north, laboring against the wind. My first thought was great blue heron because of the size and slow wing beat. Then the sun reflected off the snowy head and breast, the trailing legs resolved to extraordinary long tail feathers, and the magnificent frigatebird passed overhead at about 400', bound due south for more hospitable waters. *Christopher Letts* (SeeVols.IV:59,II:71.)

When we see a **magnificent frigatebird,** in the New York Bight or Hudson Valley, it is way off course. This large seabird is found in coastal areas of the tropical South Atlantic, only occasionally straying as far north as Chesapeake Bay. We have had three sightings in the last five years. This may represent half of all magnificent frigatebird sightings ever recorded in New York State.

4/8   Croton Point, HRM 34.5: I came upon a red-phase screech owl incubating two eggs. She was so sound asleep that my invasion did not even disturb her daily slumber. *David Karrman*

4/9   Kingston Point, HRM 92: By afternoon the day had become overcast with a light drizzle. Perhaps made even more spectacular by the gloom were the striking drake and hen red-breasted mergansers in the shallows along the shore. They were riding the chop in the face of a chilly northeast breeze. *Estell Rosen, Sidney Rosen, Steve Stanne*

Ravens   by Wayne Kocher

4/11   Tenafly, NJ, HRM 17: I watched a raven fly along the Palisades today. It landed on a ledge and was immediately mobbed by a murder of crows. Reassessing its decision, the raven took flight and continued its journey north. *Sandy Bonardi*

4/12   Poeston Kill, HRM 151.5: We were trying to net some alewives to use for striped bass bait, with little luck, in the mouth of this tidal tributary. The herring seem to be late this spring. The water temperature was 44°F—they should be here. We had to travel 66 miles south to Black Creek in Ulster County to net about three dozen alewives. *Jim Prester, the "Strictly Stripers" Club*

Croton Point, HRM 35: An immature red-headed woodpecker has been present in the north end of the park, in an oak grove, since last December. Except for some spots on its wings, the bird was pretty much in adult plumage. *Larry Bickford*

Senasqua, HRM 36: Each day I drive to Senasqua Park in early morning just to watch the river and look for birds. Today I saw two harbor seals hauled out on the beach. *Oren Smith*

4/14   Lattintown Creek, HRM 68.5: It was late afternoon and I was taking my time setting my research nets for a night session on the creek. Peak spawning activity for alewives should be near. A raccoon ambled up along the shore; he was as eager as I to see some herring. Just to the south I could see an immature bald eagle making lazy circles in the sky over the back of Cedarcliff. Many small, green flowers of the box-elder were floating in the creek, catching in my gear. *Tom Lake*

Nyack, HRM 27: Large striped bass were being caught in the Tappan Zee. We went out to pick our gillnet hoping for a bucket of alewives to use for bait. The net was full of alewives but most were minus their heads. Many had long, deep scrapes on their sides. Harbor seals! *Paul Stanton, Bob Gabrielson* [See Nyack, Vol.II:11.]

4/15 Coxsackie Creek, HRM 127: *Dan Duvall* and I had our herring research net set in the creek on a rapidly rising afternoon tide. We had not seen any alewives yet and didn't expect to see any with the water temperature at 49°F. We were intercepting a run of female yellow perch who were so ripe that they extruded strings of yellow eggs. A sudden commotion in our net told us that we had caught something other than yellow perch. We quickly waded out and discovered that we had snagged two northern pike. As we gently removed them from the net, we realized that we had caught a spawning pair. Both the female (657 mm) and the male (755 mm) were releasing eggs and sperm, respectively, a condition that fisheries biologists call running ripe. This was certainly the right time of the year and time of day to see spawning pike, but the literature describes pike as spawning over submerged vegetation. There was certainly no submerged vegetation in Coxsackie Creek and, in fact, I can't imagine where one would find that habitat in the tidal Hudson in April. Could these pike be spawning in vain? Without the appropriate habitat, would the young have a chance? *Bob Schmidt*

On most coastlines of the world there are two high and two low **tides** each day. The day referred to is not the solar day; it is the lunar day, the 24-hour-and-51-minute average interval between successive moonrises. The tides are produced by gravitational and centrifugal forces generated primarily between the moon and the earth, with some refinements added by the sun.

Poughkeepsie, HRM 75: For the drift fisherman, there can be a significant variance between night tides and day tides in terms of catch. Today we caught 14 roe shad and 7 bucks on the day drift. Tonight, making the same drift, we caught just one roe shad. *John Mylod, Bud Tschudin*

Commercial fishing gear for American shad is divided into two categories: fixed and non fixed. In the shallower areas of the river, where nets would hang down if not fixed in place, gillnet must be anchored or attached to stakes driven into the bottom. In areas of deep water, where anchoring would be impractical or impossible, nets are drifted with the current.

Raccoon   by Esther Kiviat

4/16 Senasqua, HRM 36: It was afternoon and we were walking the widening beach on the ebb tide. Just offshore something popped its round, brown, whiskered head out of the water. And then it dove. Though we stayed and looked, it was not seen again. Harbor seal? Beaver? Otter? *Marianne Murray, Bill Murray*

Town of Wappinger, HRM 67: Shadbush along the river was in bloom. This was the same date as 1997, but 17 days later than last year. *Tom Lake*

4/17 Senasqua, HRM 36: At 6:00 PM we spotted an immature beaver walking on the beach at Senasqua. The dark brown animal with its distinctive paddle was alone. *Steve Smith, Carolyn Lavallee* (This may have been the "round, brown, whiskered head" seen the previous day at this spot.)

4/18 Poughkeepsie, HRM 75: In a day drift we caught a dozen shad, all roe. It has been a slow season thus far. We saw our first osprey of the spring, circling in a southwest breeze over the river. The water was 48°F. *John Mylod, Bud Tschudin*

Roes and bucks are colloquial names given to female and male fish, generally during the spawning season. In the Hudson River it is applied almost

7

exclusively to herring: alewives, bluebacks, and American shad. *Henry Gourdine* kept meticulous logs of his commercial fishing operations for 25 years. He developed a shorthand for recording many of the fish he caught that included *"BUX"* for the male shad.

4/19   Town of Esopus, HRM 88: The shadbush was in bloom everywhere. *Fran Drakert, Bill Drakert*

Sandy Hook, NJ: Our shadbush came into bloom today on Sandy Hook. *Dery Bennett*

4/20   Poughkeepsie, HRM 75: We had a decent drift today: 26 shad, mostly roe. That was offset by the sixty striped bass that had to be carefully removed and tossed back. As April wears on, there has been an incremental increase in cormorants. We watched a long log floating in the river today. It was lined with cormorants. Water temperature was 48°F. *John Mylod, Bud Tschudin*

4/21   Wappinger Creek, HRM 67.5: Shadbush was peak, the creek banks along the tidewater reach were adorned in white. Near the head of tide, an army of dip-netters told us that this was the first day they had seen alewives—the herring were three weeks late. In the clear water shallows at low tide, we could see long, lemon-yellow spirals of yellow perch eggs. Water temperature was 49°F. *Sandy Sprague, Lawson Upchurch, Tom Lake*

Esopus Meadows, HRM 87: We went for a walk in Esopus Meadows Park and, although the birding was slow, the spring wildflowers made up for it: troutlily, hepatica, bloodroot, rue anemone, coltsfoot, violets, and rock cress. *Fran Drakert, Bill Drakert*

4/24   Green Island, HRM 153: The first American shad of the season showed up today, on their spawning run, and we began to take them in good numbers on shad darts. *Jim Prester, the "Strictly Stripers" Club*

Sport fishing for American shad requires resolve; the big-water Hudson can be intimidating. A general rule for shad fishing, which they feel no obligation to follow, is to fish inshore on the flood tide, and offshore on the ebb tide. Try docks, piers, jetties, boat launches or other points of land that have access to fairly deep water.

One of the attractions of shad fishing is its simplicity. Shorebound anglers do just about as well as those in boats. The amount and sophistication of the gear are minimal. Red, white, and yellow shad darts (leadhead jigs) are the most popular lures, although anything small and shiny will work. Six-pound monofilament line and a medium spinning outfit comprise a balanced outfit. If you use four-pound test, striped bass, carp, or a big shad may break your line. A long-handled landing net is essential. Your chances are about 50% that you will bring a hooked shad to net—they are incredible fighters, runners, and leapers. Since shad strike a lure on sight, dawn to dusk is the best time to fish for them. Persistence is the key; every shadless cast gets you one closer to a hook up and fight that you will never forget.

Little Stony Point, HRM 55: I had been seeing ravens around Bull Hill just to the north, adjacent to Little Stony Point, the last few weeks. They surely must be breeding up there as today I saw one fly over carrying nesting material in its beak. *Rich Anderson*

Croton Point, HRM 34.5: I was exploring a new trail that leads to two small pools in the woods that border the west end of the Point. In the undergrowth, a dark-feathered bird about the size of a blue jay took two short flights with a low "chuck" call giving the impression that it might have been injured. It flushed and flew low over one of the ponds revealing the distinctive shape of a nightjar. It was a chuck- will's-widow, a very rare bird for Westchester County. *Larry Bickford*

Yonkers, HRM 18: We watched a cormorant diving in the water at the mouth of the Saw Mill River. It surfaced with a ten-inch white sucker in its bill and then continued to dive several more times with the fish in its jaws. We were amazed when the cormorant finally swallowed this oversized fish. We think we heard it burp from across the water. The Hudson River Sloop *Clearwater* was at the dock and we saw several small (90 mm) spotted hake they had captured in their otter trawl. The river temperature was 55°F. *Bob Walters, Toby McAfee*

4/25 Esopus Creek, HRM 102: I tried fishing the lower Esopus for herring with a dip net. The only one catching any alewives were the osprey. Climbing to two hundred feet in the air, they would plummet at bone-breaking speeds. Upon hitting the water they would disappear for a second and then take flight, more often than not with a herring thrashing and flashing in their talons. *Noah Wadden*

   Yonkers, HRM 18: We had set a fyke net in the mouth of the Saw Mill River to sample for herring. When we went to check the net, we saw that we had managed to trap a few white perch and a cormorant! The bird had entered the open end of the net in pursuit of the perch and had become trapped itself. It was not a happy camper. We cut a hole in the net and released it. *Bob Walters, Jim Capossella, Edwin Ortega*

Ocean **salinity**, at this latitude in the Western Atlantic, is 32-35 parts-per-thousand (ppt). Throughout the year, the Hudson estuary's salinity is diluted depending upon the volume of freshwater flow from the upland watershed. In the aftermath of a prolonged storm or Adirondack snowmelt, salinity may be very low all the way south to New York Harbor's Upper Bay. At times of drought, you can taste salt in the water (> 3.0 ppt) seventy miles upriver. Salt water is denser than freshwater so the bottom of the river is generally saltier than the surface water.

4/27 Coxsackie Creek, HRM 127: We were looking for evidence of river herring spawning in the creek by setting rectangular drift nets in the current to try and capture fish larvae. While we will not know if we caught any herring eggs or larvae until we get back to the laboratory, we did see 10-15 "glass eels" in the nets. *Bob Schmidt, Dan Duvall*

Glass eels, sometimes called elvers, is one of the juvenile life stages of the American eel. Elvers arrive by the millions in the estuary each spring following a year-long journey from the Sargasso Sea, near Bermuda, where they are born. "Glass eel" is a colloquial name, owing to their near transparency. These are juvenile American eels returning to the North American estuaries of their ancestors. In anywhere from 12-30 years, depending upon their sex, they will leave the river for the sea where they will spawn once and then die.

4/28 Troy, HRM 154: *Pat Festa* and I angled at the head of the estuary below the locks of the federal dam as part of an American shad hooking mortality experiment with the U.S. Fish and Wildlife Service. We caught nearly four score shad. Shortnose sturgeon were also abundant and doing the same spring thing as the shad. *Walt Keller*

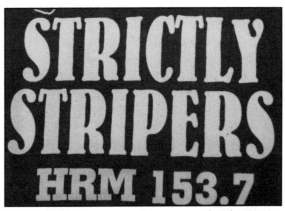

Strictly Stripers   by Jim Prester

   Coxsackie Creek, HRM 127: While we were tending to our river herring research nets in the creek an osprey was patrolling overhead. He would not fly past us but he did make frequent appearances low to the water. At one point a red-tailed hawk appeared overhead. The osprey flew up and harassed the red-tail until it left. We were not catching any alewives but we were learning a lot about hawks. *Bob Schmidt, Dan Duvall*

   Chelsea, HRM 65.2: With a warm sun under intense blue skies, the river temperature reached 50°F on the midmorning flood tide. This was about a week behind last spring and the shad and herring were likewise tardy in their spawning runs. In a 2-hour drift we caught 15 American shad—only 1 buck, and 14 roe. *Tom Lake, Christopher Letts*

Montrose, HRM 38.5: I spotted a male polyphemus moth near the river at the Montrose Veteran's Hospital. This seemed like an early hatching of this giant silk moth, as saturnids normally emerge in May and June. *Doug Rod*

Croton Point, HRM 35: The morning calm after a gale of wind yesterday. I walked along the bluff on the north side of the Point at the edge of the oak grove and noticed a wide fan of small feathers and down. As I neared a large black oak the fan narrowed and the feathers increased in size and number. Directly under the oak was the apex of the fan, a rosette of primary, secondary and tail feathers. In the center of the rosette were the iridescent head and neck of a drake mallard. This oak is a noted bald eagle perch. *Christopher Letts*

4/29 West Shokan, HRM 92: A pair of myrtle, or yellow-rumped warblers, evidently in courtship, were warbling back and forth in a tree at the confluence of the Maltby Hollow Brook and the Bushkill. *Jane Bierhorst*

4/30 Town of Esopus, HRM 88: Apple, dogwood, and lilac were coming into bloom. It is amazing how quickly the world becomes green in the last week of April. *Fran Drakert, Bill Drakert*

Fall Kill, HRM 75.5: Three large female white suckers moved upstream from the river on the start of the flood tide, its surge accentuated by the full moon and the near total lack of freshwater runoff. We were in a drought. Alewives were doing figure eights over the gravely bottom, the females spewing their amber eggs, the males covering them with milt. I had a short gillnet set obliquely to the current to catch a few herring for aging and other research data. As I watched through the clear, four-foot-deep water a large school of spottail shiners swept downstream to the river, their narrow bodies slipping neatly through the 2½" openings of the net. *Tom Lake*

Hudson Valley: This has been the driest April in this century, and the second driest in the lower Northeast since 1826. For Ulster County, it was the fourth driest April in the last 104 years. *National Weather Service, John Thompson, Mohonk Lake Cooperative Research Station*

1st Commercially-caught Hudson River American Shad

Year	Date	Water
1999	Apr 10	45°
1998	Mar 30	48°
1997	Apr 3	44°
1996	Apr 2	43°
1995	Mar 29	48°
1994	Apr 18	48°

Shad lovers   by Tom Lake

May 1999

As of now, the biological productivity of the lower Hudson is staggering. Fishes are there by the millions, with marine and freshwater species often side by side in the same patch of water. All told, the populations of fishes utilizing the lower Hudson for spawning, nursery, or feeding grounds comprise the single greatest wildlife resource in New York State.

Robert H. Boyle, *The Hudson River, a natural and unnatural history*

5/1   Green Island, HRM 153: A full "striper" moon (4/30) lit the river for some heavy striped bass action! The best shore fishing is at night and we caught and released seven bass, topped by a 28 pound, 38" striper that took my lure. Water temperature was 48°F. Daytime anglers were taking plenty of American shad. *Jim Prester, the "Strictly Stripers" Club*

Snapping turtle   by Esther Kiviat

Lattintown Creek, HRM 68.5: On the flood tide, several snapping turtles slipped silently into our gillnets and left them with large holes and fish heads. The holes were from their rummaging; the heads left from the fish eaten. Female white suckers seemed to be the favorite. As I surveyed the damage at first light, a green heron flew past, my first of the spring, and four turkey vultures sat nervously in their night roost, a dead black willow, thirty feet overhead. The last thing they wanted was to have to move.

With air temperatures in the high thirties, I could almost hear the creaks and groans of their bones as they anxiously bobbed on their branches from one foot to the other. Turkey vultures usually rise by midmorning when the sun has created thermals to assist them in gaining loft. These vultures eyed me warily. Ordinarily they would never let me get so close. I cleared the net of fish parts, giving the vultures an occasional glance. They were hunched over like black Halloween props and they could stand the tension no longer. Dropping down out of the tree, they labored toward the river lighting into another dead black willow about 150' away. I could almost hear their sigh of relief. *Tom Lake*

5/2   Poughkeepsie, HRM 75: With lilacs blooming along the river, we went for a morning shad drift. We had a decent catch: 33 roe, 5 bucks, and one surprise, a 30" shortnose sturgeon. The water temperature hit 50°F. *John Mylod, Bud Tschuden*

Croton Marsh, HRM 34: The tide was very low. I spotted a disturbance in a shallow stream of draining water and focused the spotting scope on it. I anticipated a stranded carp but saw a large snapping turtle plowing along with just the crest of the carapace, and now and then the head, in view. A flight of seven snowy egrets swept in to land about a hundred feet away. They began to skitter and scamper toward the turtle along the margin of the channel. I wished for a camera and felt my tension increase as the birds neared the turtle, which was no longer moving. The birds made a narrow detour around the turtle, kept on their way, and I breathed deeply. *Christopher Letts*

5/4   Croton River, HRM 34: I was fishing about a mile above the head of tide. The Croton was running "spring full" but not flooding. Within twenty minutes, across a 150' reach of river, I caught 3 gizzard shad, 2 rock bass, a smallmouth bass, and a 13" brook trout. The Croton River is an endlessly fascinating three-mile-long interface between the deep, cold Croton Reservoir and the fecund Croton Bay at the Hudson River. On this day there were scores if not hundreds of gizzard shad below a low dam; none was attempting to leap it but many were nosing into the froth below. They all appeared to be about 17" long and weigh about two pounds. The brook trout was long and sleek, and it weighed only 13 oz. *Jim Capossela*

Gizzard shad are not native to the Hudson River. J.R. Greeley of the New York State Conservation Department did not find them in the lower Hudson during his biological survey (Greeley 1937). It is unclear how they arrived here. Some biologists suspect an introduction from Delaware Bay via salt water; others look to the Erie Canal, Mohawk River, and other canals as a possible conduit from the Great Lakes and the Mississippi River refugium where they are native. The gizzard shad population in the estuary is reproducing at an exponential rate to a point where their biomass is becoming a concern with some fisheries scientists. Although Eagles favor gizzard shad, to a human palate, unlike the American shad and other river herring, they are not a tasty fish.

5/5   Sandy Hook, NJ: The beach plum bushes were in bloom. It is a time we celebrate with our annual beach plum jelly, cream cheese and crackers party. It is made later in the season, but I always save a jar of beach plum jelly for this day each May. *Pam Carlsen, Dery Bennett*

5/6   Tivoli North Marsh, HRM 100.5: I took my skiff into Tivoli Marsh at 5:30 PM. Compared to the tumultuous river, entering the marsh was like coming into a peaceful new world. The chatter of blackbirds, the whine of wood ducks, the quack of mallards, and the honk of geese filled my ears. Around the first bend in the creek I was startled by a pair of wood ducks; the next bend revealed a beaver

gnawing on a sapling. A while later I came upon a Canada goose sitting on its nest. The goose made quite a racket when I came past. As I was leaving, at 6:15, a flock of more than thirty wood ducks erupted from the water as I rounded a bend in the tidal creek. The air quickly filled with the whooshing and whistling of wings. *Noah Wadden*

Ulster County: Small frogs, evidently cricket frogs, were jumping into the water of a remote lake, where cricket frogs had not previously been documented. The occurrence was confirmed six weeks later, on June 21, by *Jesse Jaycox,* a naturalist for the New York Natural Heritage Program. Results: fifteen individuals seen, ten heard, one captured and photographed (and released) at the northern edge of the frog's range in North America. *John Bierhorst*

Poughkeepsie, HRM 73: *John Mylod* caught a 24½", six pound striped bass in his shad net. It had a NYSDEC tag. This bass had been tagged and released nearly three years earlier on June 19, 1996 in Little Neck Bay, Long Island Sound. It was 19" when released. This was another example of the close relationship between the Hudson, Long Island Sound, and the Atlantic.

South Lattintown Creek, HRM 68.5: The tidewater reach of this creek was lined with marsh marigolds, aglow in yellow splendor. A half-dozen least sandpipers landed, foraged along the tideline for 15 minutes, and then left. They were probably migrating through. *Tom Lake*

5/7   Annsville Creek, HRM 43.5: Almost any form of research on the estuary in springtime takes you into a world of vibrant color and sweet sounds. As I waded out to set my river herring nets, I could hear the songs and see the color of orioles, mostly the yellowish-orange of the females, in nearly every tree. *Tom Lake*

Tenafly, NJ, HRM 17: It was a day for songbirds at the Greenbrook Sanctuary. We spotted a warbling vireo, chestnut-sided warbler, prairie warbler, northern waterthrush, red-eyed vireo, yellow warbler, scarlet tanager, and a worm-eating warbler. *Nancy Slowik*

Flowering dogwood   by Esther Kiviat

5/8   Bowdoin Park, HRM 68: We huddled in the light rain along a narrow, wooded ridgeline forty feet over the Hudson River. Our *Dutchess Community College* archaeology students, carefully excavating with trowels, uncovered a tight circle of river cobbles six inches below the surface. It was an ancient hearth. Nearby several projectile points were found dating, stylistically, to about 4,000 years ago. One, a Normanskill point, had a broken tip. Ten feet away, *Jim Kennedy* found the broken tip. It had been discarded long ago. Our thoughts went back to a day in May when Native Americans sat on this prominence roasting shad, herring, and other river fish. *Stephanie Roberg-Lopez, Phyllis Lake, Tom Lake*

Normanskill is not the name of any particular Hudson Valley Indian group. For a few centuries, 4,000 years ago, Native Americans living along the Hudson and eastern Mohawk rivers made projectile points that archaeologists have stylistically labeled as *"Normanskill."* These people were likely hunter-gatherer-foragers. Other than analyzing their stone tools, we know very little of the people who made them. The style is named after Normanskill Creek, a Hudson River tributary (HRM 143.5) in Albany County.

Annsville Creek, HRM 43.5: I had set a pair of river herring research nets out in the creek three hours earlier under a blue sky. Now it was time to go get them before the tide got too deep. Halfway through the first net the sky went black and a cold curtain of rain came across the bay. Within seconds there were pyrotechnics all around and the accompanying booms were following closely. There I was with a net and a half to go, each filled with white perch and white suckers—difficult to extract under the best of circumstances—wondering how long I had to live. I never worry too much about these things; I chalk them up as adventures, *Almanac* stuff. But this morning I was worried. I gathered everything—nets, fish, anchors—and waded directly to shore across some muck that was nearly knee-deep. I was 300' from safety . . . , then 200 . . . , then 100, wondering what it would be like to hear the crack and feel the juice. I plunged headlong into a large stand of phragmites where I waited out the storm for the next twenty minutes. I was soaked, cold, weary, but alive. *Tom Lake*

5/9   Minerva, HRM 284: The shadbush along Moxham Pond, which drains to Minerva Brook, Trout Brook, the Scroon River and the Hudson, bloomed today, a little later than last year (April 20). *Mike Corey*, Sue Corey

Poughkeepsie, HRM 75: *John Mylod* caught a 24" male striped bass, carrying a tag, in his shad net—his second tag recovery in three days. The bass had been tagged and released August 2, 1996 at Norwalk, Connecticut, in Long Island Sound.

Nyack, HRM 27: On Mother's Day morning *Bob Gabrielson* found an 18" summer flounder and a 24" weakfish in his herring net. They would be dinner for Bob and his wife, Joan.

5/10 Croton River, HRM 34: Since November, all daytime low tides at the mouth of the Croton River have been eagerly awaited by the gulls. As soon as the mudflats are exposed, the ring-billed gulls start clamming. By the score they stroll over the flats discerning the presence of the wedge clam—who knows how? Clam in beak, they fly over the Croton-Harmon commuter parking lot, dropping the clam to break it upon the pavement (and sometimes bombing a vehicle when the lot is crowded). Drop height must be carefully judged: too high and the waiting herring and black-backed gulls pirate the meat; too low and the clam does not break. By this spring the lot is covered with the crushed shells of many thousands of clams. This morning I watched a mixed flock of killdeer and least sandpipers enjoying a rare favor from their enemies the gulls. They were filling up on crushed shell, calcium that would shortly aid in forming eggshells when they reached their breeding grounds. *Christopher Letts*

For information on the New York State Breeding Bird Atlas visit on the Internet: http://www.dec.state.ny.us/website/dfwmr/wildlife/bba/index.html

Yonkers, HRM 18: We went seining with students from the preschool class from *Christ the King School* in Yonkers at the Beczak Center beach on the river. Among our catch were sand shrimp, Atlantic blue crabs, young-of-the-year *(yoy)* Atlantic tomcod (30 mm), northern pipefish, and a few mud crabs. Salinity was 6.5 ppt; water temperature was 63°F. *David Rosenfeld*

Young-of-the-year aptly describes the multitude of recently hatched aquatic fauna found in the Hudson River each spring, summer and fall. The progeny of tomcod, shad, river herring, striped bass, white perch, blue crabs, shrimp, jellyfish, and many others, are present by the millions. So many references are made of their presence that scientists have taken to

abbreviating the phrase to *yoy,* shorthand for young-of-the-year.

5/11 Green Island, HRM 153: Shore fishing for stripers had slacked off. The boys in the boats were seeing all the action. Two of them told me that they had caught and released 27 bass, to 32 pounds, up against the falls of the federal dam. It was "catch them while you can." The Coast Guard had yet to put in the "off limits" buoys to keep anglers away from the plunge pool and rough water just below the dam. Water temperature was 49°F. *Jim Prester, the "Strictly Stripers" Club*

Pete Seeger   by Tom Lake

Coxsackie Creek, HRM 127.5: The tide was very low at sundown. We set our gillnet to sample river herring in a pool, 3½' deep, just to see what might be hanging around. By the time it got dark, we had caught nine alewives, as well as yellow perch, white suckers, and redbreast sunfish. We were also setting some drift nets to sample for herring eggs and larvae when we saw several alewives zip past us heading upstream. Forty minutes later we got back to our herring net and, in the light of our lantern, we could not see the top seamline. As we pulled the nearshore end, we discovered why: a thirty-pound snapping turtle. The turtle had been attracted by the 51 alewives we caught in our 51' net (5 females, 46 males). *Bob Schmidt, Rick Banducci*

Esopus Meadows. HRM 87: Dogwood was in peak bloom along the river. *Fran Drakert, Bill Drakert*

Little Stony Point, HRM 55: We were walking the trails when suddenly we heard a whir of wings and saw a flash of birds overhead. A mourning dove had settled safely to the ground as a peregrine falcon was pulling up from its stoop. I guess we all felt fortunate to have seen the falcon, including the dove. *Rich Anderson, John Zuvic, Joe Diebboll*

Stooping is a term that is used by birders to describe a dive. Webster's Dictionary defines it as "to dive down swiftly; to attack prey."

Tenafly, NJ, HRM 17: A Tennessee warbler came by today along with two Lincoln's sparrows. *Nancy Slowik*

5/12 Indian Kill, HRM 85: We were canoeing inland from tidewater, under the railroad trestle, when we spotted a large orange and white koi swimming ahead of us in the shallow water. This variety of carp has been found previously in the Indian Kill. *Bob Schmidt, Dan Duvall* (See Vol.V:19.)

Koi, also known as **sanke**, is a domesticated variety of the common carp *(Cyprinus carpio)*. Koi are sold in pet shops for private ponds. When these ponds overflow, or the owners get tired of caring for them, they can end up in the Hudson River where they live long and grow large.

South Lattintown Creek, HRM 68.5: We were clearing our herring gillnet in a mid-afternoon ebb tide about three-quarters of a mile from the Hudson. I saw a turtle moving slowly upstream along the bottom and, unable to

identify it in four feet of water, I cradled it in the bottom seamline and hauled it up. It was a wood turtle, measuring 218 mm carapace length. We took some photos and released the turtle where it was captured. This size is at the high end for the species, indicating a very old turtle. After some initial reconnoitering, the turtle continued upstream. We followed it, at a distance. At this point the creek varied from 10"-18" deep. Every thirty feet the turtle would stop, brace itself on a rock or submerged branch, rise up on its hind legs with its head out of the water, look around, get its bearings (we assumed), submerge, and be on its way. We finally went back to our net when the turtle moved into the eddy of an undercut bank, into a catch basin. It may have been looking for a place to rest. At this point, South Lattintown Creek is about 35' wide at high tide and 15' wide at low tide. It has a primary substrate of fine to coarse gravels, interspersed with gray clay sediments where the current is less pronounced. Primary vegetation on the tide flats is yellow pond lily with some soft-stemmed bulrush and arrow arum. The adjacent low marsh is primarily cattail and phragmites. The high marsh area has marsh marigold. The canopy is strictly hardwood, dominated by box elder and black willow *Tom Lake, Phyllis Lake*

Tenafly, NJ, HRM 17: Pink ladyslipper was in bloom and two more spring warblers made an appearance: a Blackburnian and a Wilson's warbler. *Nancy Slowik*

5/14 Vloman Kill, HRM 138: We canoed a short distance up the Vloman Kill to sample for river herring. Our sets lasted about twenty minutes and we managed to catch our first blueback herring of the season. Most bluebacks are on their way to the Mohawk River, via the Erie Canal, to spawn. We also caught sixty white perch, which are dreadfully difficult to remove from a gillnet. Several birds chided us from some tall cottonwoods. When they flew off, we saw very pointed, bent wings—nighthawks! *Robert Schmidt, Alec Schmidt*

Tenafly, NJ, HRM 17: Another spring day, another warbler, this time a blackpoll. A pearl crescent butterfly was also seen. *Nancy Slowik*

Hudson River Fisheries Unit   by DEC

5/15   Eddyville, HRM 92: We had run out of striper bait while fishing Rondout Creek. We beached our boat just below the dam at Eddyville and I cautiously walked up along the rocks, dip net in hand, looking for herring. There was much activity in the pools beneath the dam and I thought they might be alewives. To my surprise, flush up against the face of the dam, I saw hundreds, if not thousands, of shad. Gizzard shad. They had come upstream as far as they could go. As the tide continued to drop, they milled about in large schools, half out of the water—their backs exposed—looking for a way up and over. I never did find any herring for striper bait. *Joe Diamond, Denis Moran*

Dobbs Ferry, HRM 23: Using a thirty-foot seine, we hauled three times in quick succession within fifty feet of the beach. We caught approximately 150 herring. Two of the herring (62 and 64 mm) looked somehow different. They were not the usual herring we see in the lower Hudson. *Jim Capossela, Bob Walters*

We identified these "different" herring using a microscope to count their gill rakers (to differentiate them from other Hudson river herrings). These two herring had 32-33 gill rakers on the lower limb of the first arch. This number is too few for blueback herring (41-52), American shad (59-73), or alewife (36); it was too many for hickory shad (18-23). Juvenile Atlantic herring of this size have 25-36 gill rakers. Several other measurements, such as the placement of their dorsal fin, also pointed to these being **Atlantic herring**. While there are other annotated records of juvenile Atlantic herring in the Hudson River (HRM 14-42), this occurrence can be considered rare. These were probably marine strays from a fall 1998 year class, spawned in the New York Bight (Jones 1978:112). *Tom Lake*

5/16   South Lattintown Creek, HRM 68.5: For two days we had super high tides. Each morning, high water spilled over into the flood plain of Lattintown Creek and into the forest along the edge. I cannot remember ever seeing tides any higher. Unfortunately, the tides didn't bring many river herring in with them. Last night I had to wear a life jacket at half tide to bob out and check the nets. The air was sweet; Dame's Rocket was in bloom. There was no moon but all the stars were out. Spawning carp were jumping in the flooded pond lilies. In the dark, they sounded like intermittent cannons going off. At midnight I was out again waist-deep in the water. I heard a squawk and looked downstream. A great blue heron, flying low over the water, was coming right at me. It flared off just a bit as it passed, its silhouette looking very primeval in the black of night—very pterosaur-like. I did not know that great blues flew at night. It vocalized for several minutes, in several different tones. I also did not know that they had such a variety of sounds. Solo night duty on research nets can be tedious. I slept a bit, drank too much coffee, did two crosswords, and after two hours went back out and cleared the nets again. The tide was slowly ebbing and I found more white suckers, white perch, 2 alewives, and 5 huge snapping turtles in the net. One had a white perch, another had a white sucker, and the other three were just very unhappy to see me. I pulled the nets out. When snapping turtles use your research nets as a buffet, the show is over. *Tom Lake*

Tenafly, NJ, HRM 17: Our first bay-breasted warbler of the spring showed up today. *Nancy Slowik*

5/17 North Germantown, HRM 109: We launched at midday at the NYSDEC boat ramp at North Germantown to go seining with the NYSDEC Hudson River Fisheries Unit. This was a survey trip to sample for striped bass and American shad. *Andy Kahnle,* a fisheries biologist, commented that the river, at 67°F, was warmer than he expected. We hauled our 500' seine once near the Ramshorn River (HRM 112.2) and once at Rogers Island (114.0). The biologists were impressed with the number of American shad and striped bass we caught; it was the most they had taken all spring. Mixed in were a few largemouth bass, one white catfish, and some big carp. Struggling with the carp wore everyone out. The air temperature was 75°F. *Megan Molique, Rick Molique*

Poughkeepsie, HRM 73: *John Mylod* caught in his shad net, his third tagged striped bass in less than three weeks. This one was 29½" long and weighed 9 pounds. It had a tag from the New Jersey Department of Environmental Protection. It had been tagged and released at 26¾" on March 28, 1995 in Delaware Bay, more than 250 miles to the south.

Lattintown Creek, HRM 68.5: In the shade of evening, a score of white suckers raced up through some riffles, through the branches of some deadfalls, and across some gravely runs to reach a quiet pool just above the reach of tide. There, males positioned themselves to either side of the females and repeatedly bumped them. This forced the females' eggs to extrude. In a quick swirl the males spun around in the

pool covering the eggs with their milt. As darkness grew there was a good chance that this pool would be visited tonight by eels and white perch looking to dine on sucker eggs. *Phyllis Lake, Tom Lake*

Croton Point, HRM 34: I found a diamondback terrapin hatchling dying on the railroad bed at the Metro North Croton rail yard. At the Croton Point Nature Center we put the tiny turtle in a brackish water tank and, before long, it had revived. *Wayne Kocher*

5/18 Coxsackie Creek, HRM 127.5: We were sampling with gillnets for adult alewives that ascend this tributary in May from the Atlantic to spawn. We caught no adults but we did retrieve two small alewives. They measured 138 and 150 mm. These should have been yearlings, heading for their second summer at sea, based on size. The surprising thing about them though was that they were sexually mature—the larger one being a male and the smaller a female with eggs. These two fish had the morphology, growth, and size at maturity of landlocked fish, giving some credibility to *Karin Limburg's* theory that some Hudson River-spawned alewives never leave the river. *Bob Schmidt, Aime Bourdon, Casey Donohue*

Lattintown Creek, HRM 68.5: As we were setting a short gillnet in 3½' of water to catch river herring, a snapping turtle the size of a flying saucer sat on the bottom, watching us and the net, poised, waiting. Within seconds, the net caught a large white sucker. Almost immediately there was a tug-of-war between us and the alien spacecraft for that fish. *Tom Lake, Phyllis Lake*

Fort Montgomery, HRM 46.5: Heavy fog and a low ceiling covered the tip of Anthony's Nose. In a cold drizzle, I walked up along Popolopen Creek in late afternoon noticing that the flower buds of the yellow flag at the water's edge were about to bloom. I looked and listened for spawning river herring all night. I saw but a few and heard nothing. When I walked out with my gear just after first light, in a steady drizzle, the yellow flag were in bloom. *Tom Lake*

Hudson River shad bake   by Tom Lake

5/22   Nyack, HRM 27: It was a beautiful spring day with air temperatures in the low 80s. Several hundred people sampled baked, pickled, and smoked shad at our twelfth annual Nyack Shad Bake. The American shad migration was nearing its conclusion; by now most of the fish were spawning 75-125 miles upriver. The spring season for celebration of the river's bounty was winding down. *Christopher Letts, Andra Sramek, Tom Lake*

5/24   Lattintown Creek, HRM 68.5: A pair of wild turkeys led me down a trail to the creek, managing to stay a comfortable distance, for them, ahead of me. In the warm spring breeze it looked like a snowstorm as the cottonwoods released their fluffy seeds to the wind. A red eft (red-spotted newt) was sitting right at the water's edge, in the spot where I usually have my morning coffee along the creek, in the shade of a black willow. This morning I found an alternate perch. *Tom Lake*

5/25   Croton Point, HRM 34.5: On a sunny, windy day we saw two orchard orioles and two northern orioles in the trees at the base of the landfill. The flashy orange and black of the male

northern oriole was in striking contrast to the elegant reddish-brown and black of the male orchard. Bladder campion was in bloom along with yarrow, deadly nightshade, red clover, field mustard, bird's-foot trefoil, wild madder, daisies, spurge, and purple vetch. Tree swallows were snapping up insects. The thickets on the south side of the cap were full of yellow warblers and goldfinches. We heard, *"Fitzbew,"* and saw a willow flycatcher dart from a dry stalk, nab an insect in the air, return to its stalk, and swallow it. A buff-colored, streaky-breasted female bobolink was perched on some weeds with an immature male—its black, white, and yellow plumage still muted. Four monarchs and two black tiger swallowtails blew by. In the mudflats by the marsh we saw a semipalmated sandpiper and four least sandpipers. Their beaks were rapidly probing the gooey mud for invertebrates and they raced back and forth in a low tide feeding frenzy. The bobolinks were the most thrilling sighting in a bird-rich day, since their population has declined so sharply due to habitat loss. *Amy Silberkleit, Michael Shiffer, Isis Shiffer, Elijah Shiffer*

Manhattan, HRM 10: New York City Park Enforcement Patrol responded to a call for an injured animal on the banks of the Hudson in Riverside Park along the upper west side of Manhattan. New York City Park Rangers identified it as a dead harbor porpoise. Personnel from The Riverhead Foundation arrived to take the marine mammal away. *Steve Raphael*

Kim Durham, Stranding Program Director of the *Riverhead Foundation for Marine Research and Preservation*, Riverhead, NY, forwarded this information on the dead porpoise: The harbor porpoise was a male, 109 cm in length, 20.0 kg in weight. Its stomach contained 15-20 fish otoliths, species unknown. Cause of death unknown.

The **Riverhead Foundation for Marine Research and Preservation** has a 24-hour Stranding Hotline phone number. If you see a marine mammal that needs assistance, please call (631) 369-9829.

5/27 Doodletown, HRM 45.5: From the trailhead just across Route 9W from Iona Marsh, we walked up the 1777 east trail to Doodletown, a hamlet that was razed when it became part of Bear Mountain State Park in the 1960s. Honeysuckle, poison ivy, bittersweet, and grape vines obliterated the foundations we knew were there. Barberry, wineberry, and wild roses narrowed the trail. The view of Iona Marsh and the Hudson River was spectacular. The forsythia and wisteria gone wild, and the tangled thickets of berry producing vines made great habitat for nesting and migrating warblers. From the dense vegetation we heard yellow warblers and common yellowthroat, saw several male and female American redstarts—the black males showing orange feathers on their wings and tails as they darted through the branches catching insects. Near the old reservoir we heard the songs of the cerulean warbler and hooded warbler. Tiger swallowtails and pipevine swallowtails were sunning on the phlox; azure blue butterflies fluttered along the path. We surprised a blue-gray gnatcatcher darting back and forth along a fence, collecting spider silk for its nest. A thick protruding wisteria vine became a huge black rat snake, wrapped around a branch. *Amy Silberkleit, Michael Shiffer, Isis Shiffer, Elijah Shiffer*

5/29-5/31 Upper New York Harbor: Large schools of 24"-28" weakfish roamed the Upper Bay all Memorial Day weekend providing extraordinary sport for anglers. I fished for a couple hours and landed fifty, mostly on lead-headed bucktail jigs. *Glenn Blank*

5/30 Eddyville, HRM 92: Even though it was the middle of the night, a full moon bathed the shoreline in silvery light. The tide was nearing high in Rondout Creek not far from the Eddyville Dam, about three miles from the Hudson. Our pair of fifty-foot gillnets were set parallel to and ten feet offshore where we hoped migrating river herring would pass. At 2:00 AM they began, in ones and twos and threes, like slivers of moonlight flashing in the twine. In an hour we had collected 57. The Rondout is one of the few tidal Hudson River tributaries where the spawning adults of both species of river herring—alewives and blueback herring—are consistently found together. Our catch consisted of 42 alewives and 15 blueback herring. *Tom Lake, Chris Lake*

Progress of Blooms:	**Shadbush**					
County/HRM	1999	1998	1997	1996	1995	1994
Essex (302)	5/9	4/20	5/19	5/7	5/6	5/10
Warren (245)	5/1	4/10	5/9	5/2	5/2	5/3
Washington (185)	4/30	4/9	5/9	4/29	5/2	5/3
Albany (145)	4/24	4/9	5/7	4/28	4/26	4/26
Greene (113)	4/21	4/3	5/7	4/26	4/23	4/25
Ulster (88)	4/19	4/1	4/22	4/25	4/23	4/25
Orange (56)	4/16	4/1	4/21	4/26	4/23	4/24
Dutchess (67)	4/16	3/31	4/16	4/24	4/21	4/22
Putnam (52)	4/15	4/1	4/14	4/22	4/18	4/21
Westchester (35)	4/14	3/31	4/10	4/19	4/18	4/21
Sandy Hook (0)	4/19	4/8	4/17	4/28	4/25	4/25

Hikers at Mohonk

by Esther Kiviat

Summer

June 1999

You feel as though you can come to grips with the Hudson.
But then, just when you think you understand the river,
perceive its rhythms, and maybe even explain it all to someone else,
you discover something new.

Robert Boyle, *The Hudson, a natural and unnatural history*

6/1   Ulster County: A sizeable colony of Appalachian sand-wort—200 plants—was growing on exposed slabrock with pitch pine and scrub oak. The plants were a little past prime but with many blossoms still fresh. Rare in the Northeast, Appalachian sandwort is found in New York State only in the mid-Hudson region, on the west side of the river. *John Bierhorst*

6/2   Poeston Kill, HRM 151.5: We watched the flood tide roar in from the river and we hoped that blueback herring would be riding the surge. In the shadow of old Troy, we set our research nets oblique to the current and waited. Within minutes we could see flashes of silver as herring hit the net. *Aime Bourdon* tried to catch a few herring on rod and reel with a small shad dart, but only succeeded in catching smallmouth bass and striped bass. On another day these would have been a prize. *Casey Donohue, Bob Schmidt, Tom Lake*

Green Island, HRM 153.4: The anglers along the shore, "the regulars," kept telling us that the shad run was over, they had all left. For a while it seemed to be true. We caught gizzard shad (they don't count) and a few blueback herring. Then *Bob Schmidt* had his shad dart yanked hard and he was into a nice American shad. In only a minute or two he had a four-and-a-half-pound roe shad lying on the cobble beach. *Tom Lake*

6/4   Sleightsburg Spit, HRM 90: The season's water chestnut hadn't yet encroached on the shallows enough to block views of sunfish nests and the activity around them. A spit of land uncovered at low tide allowed close approach to nests in the shallowest water. Male pumpkinseed and redbreast sunfish guarded closely spaced, roughly circular patches of gravel and stones cleared of sediments and ooze. They were understandably skittish in the foot-deep, clear water given the presence of two great blue herons on the flats south of the spit. Males in adjacent nests challenged each other, flaring their gill covers to show off opercular flaps. On the redbreasts these are rather long and black; they are shorter but tipped with scarlet on the pumpkinseeds. These flaps look like eyes, a big, fierce countenance created by the flaring gill covers. The fish take their guard duties seriously, sallying forth to assail wandering sunnies, golden shiners, even a passing carp. The carp were also spawning in the shallows, creating great commotion as they thrashed about in thick patches of water chestnut. Adopting the still pose of the herons for long minutes also reveals less obvious fish—an eight-inch eel nosing about on the bottom and killifish darting from the shelter of one water chestnut rosette to the next. Unfortunately, I cannot hold that pose as long as great blues can, and as I move, the fish scatter. *Steve Stanne*

An **opercular flap** is a gill cover, a bony plate that protects the fish' gills. Fish will often flare their gill covers in response to a threat, to make themselves appear larger when guarding their nests.

Dutchess County, NY: On our way to visit an eagle nest we found wood anenome in bloom and heard wood thrush and veery singing in the forest. At the site, *Pete Nye* scaled the nest tree and carefully lowered the seven-week-old bald eaglet down from atop a 75' white pine. This male bird was hatched on April 19. With much attention, its parents wheeled and soared overhead voicing their concern at our intrusion. Below in a small clearing technicians *Craig Thompson* and *Hollie Amsler* took blood samples, banded its leg for future identification, and declared the baby bird to be fit. Within minutes the eaglet was hoisted back up into its nest, no worse for wear, to rejoin a three-foot American eel that may have been its breakfast. Before long, the adults would return to the nest as well. The adult male was also a tagged bird, having been banded in its nest as an eaglet on Massachusetts' Quabbin Reservoir in 1993. This pair had produced an egg that did not hatch in spring 1998. *Steve Lawrence, Beth Waterman, Steve Stanne, Tom Lake*

Spring 1999: The total bald eagle fledge count (new eagles) for this spring would be five. Last year's pair from Greene County that had three young had only one this year. Another pair that had one last year would fledge three this year, and this one we visited today made five.

6/5   Eddyville, HRM 92: On the start of the flood tide we saw an immature bald eagle flying up Rondout Creek to the Eddyvile Dam, probably looking for the same thing we were: blueback herring. After a couple of passes in the wind, failing to find any fish to dive on, it disappeared above the dam. We, likewise, found no herring. *Tom Lake, Phyllis Lake*

6/7   Thompson Island, HRM 193.5: Four killdeer have made their home on the Thompson Island Road. Each morning and evening as I pass, they do their best to "distract" my truck from their nests. *George Story*

Poughkeepsie, HRM 68: A record air temperature of 95°F was recorded today. *National Weather Service*

Great blue heron   by Wayne Kocher

Croton Point, HRM 34: On an incredibly hot day, while walking along the marsh, I spotted two least bitterns. It was a good day to be a wading bird. *Larry Bickford*

Newark, NJ: A record air temperature of 99°F was recorded today. *National Weather Service*

6/8   Rokeby, HRM 96.5: I saw a young black bear, sporting an orange ear tag, wandering around the area. I lost sight of it as it made its way down along the river. *Roger Downs*

6/9   Poeston Kill, HRM 151.5: From a bridge above the creek we peered down into the clear water of the rising tide. Behind a large stone we spotted a two-foot-long northern pike, a voracious predator. It faced into the current, unmoving except for the flutter of its fins to maintain position. This curious "fish-mime" was enduring the close company of three small American eels, as they slithered around and over the rocks in search of fish eggs and larvae. These brave six-inch eels may have sensed that the pike was not hungry, or they may have not noticed it at all. *Bob Schmidt, Tom Lake, Casey Donohue, Aime Bourdon*

Waterford, HRM 158: The 300' long lock of the Erie Canal's Lock 6 was teeming with adult blueback herring on their way west to the Mohawk River to spawn. As the lower, eastern gate to the lock opened to allow boats to enter, thousands of blueback herring also moved into the lock. Once inside, the gate closed and water was pumped in. At Lock 6, a fifty-foot rise in water level, the result of over three million gallons of water being pumped into the lock, occurs in just nine minutes. Once inside the lock, the herring swarm to the upstream, western end to await the opening of that gate, to continue on their way. *Bob Schmidt, Tom Lake, John Tremblay, Casey Donohue, Aime Bourdon*

6/10   Bangall, HRM 88: A young black bear, twice the size of a large dog, crossed our yard heading east. The bear had an orange tag in its left ear. *Stephanie Roberg-Lopez* (See Rokeby, 6/8.)

6/11   Roelif Jansen's Kill, HRM 111: Cruising down the river today I took a peek up the Roe-Jan. About 300 yds. upstream a bald eagle flushed from a tree. Almost immediately three crows came diving down on it. They harassed the eagle for about five minutes until an osprey showed up and began making dives on the eagle as well. For the next ten minutes I witnessed spectacular aerial combat. The two

huge birds finally vanished over a hill. *Noah Wadden*

Esopus Meadows, HRM 87: We counted 53 mute swans and two great blue herons out on the meadows. The water chestnut was all emerged so the fishermen have gone elsewhere. *Bill Drakert, Fran Drakert*

6/15   Green Island, HRM 153: The striped bass fishing never really took off this spring. It was the poorest striper fishing in 15 years. It seems to have declined every year since the January flood of 1996 (see Vol.II:89-92), when tides were as much as thirty feet above normal. No big forty-pound fish were taken this spring. The blueback herring, a major striper forage, also seem to be decreasing in both numbers and size. *Jim Prester*

Tivoli North Bay, HRM 100: There were 17 paddlers out for the tenth annual Palisades Nature Association spring canoe trip. We set out from Tivoli North Bay to Magdalen Island, just outside in the choppy river, at low tide. After lunch we returned to the marsh to the deafening sound of red-winged blackbirds and marsh wrens. *Bob Rancan, Nancy Slowik, Ross Smith*

6/16   Wallkill River, HRM 77: *Witchity-witchity-witchity* . . . the song of the common yellowthroat was decreasing from its springtime breeding peak. A great blue heron flew across the river with a slow rhythmic wing beat. The drought had parched the ground and turned the turf to dust. As I walked along the shore, I spotted a piece of gray chert protruding slightly from a crack in the dry earth. It was the thin edge of a small projectile point staring up at me, having eroded from the soil. I had found a very old Paleoindian "Clovis" point. *Tom Lake*

Note: The location of this find was registered with the New York State Museum, the New York State Department of Parks and Recreation, and the National Park Service's registry of prehistoric sites. Federal, state, and local laws prohibit the collecting of artifacts on public lands without a permit. **Clovis,** or fluted points, are somewhat rare in the Northeast. They are a diagnostic tool of the first people to enter the Hudson Valley, Paleoindians, who arrived perhaps 11,000 years ago in the late Pleistocene. The Wallkill River Valley was a passageway through Orange and Ulster counties as they followed game herds to chert quarries in Greene County and the upper Hudson. Lengthwise fluting of the stone in manufacture gives these tools a slim, distinctive look. This one had also been heat-treated in order to facilitate parallel flaking, a hallmark of fluted projectile points. Geologist *Phil La Porta* identified the lithic (stone) as a beautiful rosy-white, high quality chert, a Big Springs member of the Epler Formation. The chert had originated in a quarry near Branchville, Sussex County, NJ, 55 miles south of where it was found. This 44 mm long point was probably a small, resharpened spear tip. *Bob Funk*, New York State Archaeologist emeritus, identified it as a **Barnes**-type fluted point, a style that may have originated in Southwestern Ontario about 10,500 years ago. This point is being studied by archaeologists in an effort to further our knowledge of our ancestral Hudson Valley neighbors.

6/18   Piermont, HRM 25: *Bob Gabrielson* reported that a 13-pound bluefish was caught off the end of the Piermont Pier. It was taken on cut menhaden. Weakfish, 16"-18" long, were also being taken on bunker and bloodworms.

6/20   Tappan Zee, HRM 26: My dad's friend Butch was out fishing in the river, east of the channel just south of the Tappan Zee Bridge. In addition to a dozen white perch, he hooked and landed a glorious 22" weakfish. It was caught on bloodworms. Butch has caught 8-10 weakfish up to 25" at that spot. I filleted the weakfish and ate it. It was superb table fare. *Jim Capossela*

Summer Solstice

6/21   Waterford, HRM 158: The first *yoy* blueback herring were dimpling the surface of the Erie Canal locks. In our seine samples from Locks 3-5 we found hundreds of *yoy* white suckers smallmouth bass, largemouth bass, spottail shiners, and a dozen or more brook silverside. *Bob Schmidt, Tom Lake, John Williams, Tom Schroeder, Casey Donohue, Aime Bourdon*

6/21   Catskill Creek, HRM 113: Anglers have been catching walleye up to 27" long at Rushmore Dam at the head of tide in Catskill Creek. *Jon Powell*

Mute swan   by Esther Kiviat

6/22   Tarrytown, HRM 27: This afternoon the river looked like an illustration from *A Child's First Book of Transportation*. A silver train shot along the Westchester shore; a tug called the *Barker Girls* powered upriver with a crew member sitting in the stern on a mess of chain; an Army helicopter whacked its way north toward West Point; the rumble of jets could be heard far overhead; traffic was slow on the Tappan Zee Bridge; a skidoo laid white icing on the water; our small sailboat and, taking it all in, pedestrians walking along the shore. *Daniel Wolff, Lorenzo Wolff*

6/24   North Germantown, HRM 109: The warm water of the rising tide was teeming with *yoy* blueback herring (20 mm). An osprey flew overhead. With all these fish, it was a good time of the year to be an osprey. *Bob Schmidt, Tom Lake, Casey Donohue, Aime Bourdon*

Poughkeepsie, HRM 75.5: Since April, the Hudson Valley had received only 30% (5.4") of its normal fifty-year average rainfall (17.8"). *National Weather Service*

Nutten Hook, HRM 124: We seined the extensive inshore shallows looking for river herring. The warm (76°F) water was filled with *yoy* blueback herring, alewives, striped bass, and spottail shiners. We had no problem finding and setting our net around thousands of them. Our only problem was that most of the herring were so small they slipped right through the quarter-inch mesh of our seine. *Bob Schmidt, Tom Lake, Casey Donohue, Aime Bourdon*

6/29 Upper Nyack, HRM 28: Oppressive heat. The morning paper headlined a water shortage. In late afternoon a Hudson Valley "bowler of a thunderstorm" cracked right over our heads. When it passed I went for a swim and the first black-crowned night heron I'd seen this year landed on a rotting pier to look things over. *Daniel Wolff, Lorenzo Wolff*

6/30 Esopus Meadows, HRM 87: We picked black raspberries today but this year's crop is a great disappointment. There were many berries but almost all of them were too small to bother with. I guess the lack of rain did them in. Black raspberries are great but I barely got enough to improve two bowls of cereal. *Fran Drakert and Bill Drakert*

Mid-Hudson Valley: June 1999 was the second warmest and fourth driest June in the last 104 years. *John Thompson, Mohonk Lake Cooperative Research Station*

Red eft (red-spotted newt) by Esther Kiviat

July 1999

Geologically, the Hudson River, like the Grand Canyon,
is an open book of the history of the earth, although some of the
pages are torn and a few chapters are missing.

Robert H. Boyle, *The Hudson, a natural and unnatural history*

7/2   New Hamburg, HRM 68.5: We had timed our arrival at Bowdoin Park perfectly. The tide in the marsh was low. Our *Vassar College* Summers Scholars were investigating an archaeological site that had been dry ground 4,000 years ago, but had now been claimed by a rise in sea level. We wet-screened the sediments (mud!) and found a few hammerstones and some fire-cracked rock, evidence of a former Native American presence. Clouds of banded killifish and a few blue crabs filled the many shallow depressions that held water on the tide flats. They were waiting for the next tide to rise and set them free. *Jon Herzog, Melissa Gallo, Asia Flemister, Lauren Dalrymple, Sara Winchombe, Tom Lake, Stephanie Roberg-Lopez*

Vassar College Summer Scholars   by Phyllis Lake

7/3   Poughkeepsie, HRM 74: I heard my first cicadas today, a sound that commands attention. When you hear them for the first time that *is* the first time. Theirs is not a sound that you suddenly hear and wonder how long it has been going on. *John Mylod*

7/5   New Hamburg, HRM 68.5: It was another hot day of excavating at Bowdoin Park. The summer heat had arrived; at midday it was 99°F. with a heat index of 114°. We moved into the shade of the woods to dig. From what is considered the "colonial plow zone," a kaolin pipe fragment appeared in our screen. At a slightly lower level we found some flakes of brown jasper. The maker's mark on the clay pipe identified its origin as 18th century Dutch. The jasper may have been considerably older. These were percussion flakes produced by a Native American during the creation of a stone tool. *Tom Lake, Bonnie Bogumil, Rachel Harris, Danielle Diamaiolo, Amanda daSilva, Tim Jones, George Doere*

Heat index is a cumulative measure of discomfort. It takes into account both air temperature and relative humidity. A heat index that exceeds about 90°F is quite uncomfortable. On this day, while the air temperature was 99°, the added effect of the humidity made the "apparent temperature" 114°.

   Manhattan, HRM 5: A record air temperature of 101°F was registered today replacing the old record for the date of 98°. *National Weather Service*

7/6   Albany, HRM 145: A record air temperature of 99°F was recorded today in the state capitol replacing the old record of 92°. *National Weather Service*

   Manhattan, HRM 5: For the second day in a row, a record air temperature, 101°F, was registered. This replaced the old record for the date of 98°. *National Weather Service*

7/7   Yonkers, HRM 18: The Northeast Recreation Association went seining with us at the Beczak Center beach on the river this morning. We captured and released a softshell blue crab and several sand shrimp. Among the fish taken were Atlantic silverside and *yoy* bluefish. We were unable to identify one fish in our catch. It was elongate, 80 mm in length, with a protruding mouth full of prominent teeth, and a forked tail [inshore lizardfish]. Salinity was 11.0 ppt; water temperature was 80°F. *David Rosenfeld*

Inshore lizardfish look like brightly striped and mottled cigars. A favorite of snorkelers, they grow to 18" and favor the tropical and temperate waters of the Atlantic. Lizardfish are a voracious predator that lurks in the shallows, burrowing in the bottom sediments to ambush passing prey. Larval lizardfish are frequently carried into the Hudson Estuary on summer flood tide currents. Subsequently, juvenile lizardfish are occasionally found in late summer and fall in the brackish waters of the lower Hudson.

Sloop Sojourner Truth   by Tom Lake

7/8   Yonkers, HRM 18: We went seining with students from *Public School 7* from the Bronx at the Beczak Center beach on the river. In our net were sand shrimp, northern pipefish, and many comb jellies. The most interesting catch was a small *yoy* bluefish with a semicircular bite where its tail had been. This fish had likely fallen victim to the sharp teeth of

one of its larger "siblings." Salinity was 9.7 ppt; water temperature was 78°F. *David Rosenfeld*

Nyack, HRM 28: *Bob Gabrielson* was still catching adult bluefish and weakfish in his "bunker net." When he pulled his net today, there were only a few menhaden, but he did find dinner: a 13-pound bluefish and an 8-pound weakfish.

Bunker nets are short (fifty to one-hundred-feet-long) 3½"-mesh gillnets used to catch Atlantic menhaden. Menhaden are a marine herring that use the lower, brackish estuary by the millions each summer and fall, as a nursery and feeding ground. They are known colloquially as "bunker," or "mossbunker."

7/9   Newcomb Lake, HRM 300: At an elevation of 1736', Newcomb Lake in the High Peaks of the Adirondacks is another remote source of the Hudson River. On this clear summer day at Fish Rock lean-to, it was an extraordinary place of quiet, perfectly composed and benign, excepting the deerflies—"Worst in forty years," says *Andy Blanchette* of Newcomb. Every green thing was arranged just so: a stalk out of water with white seed head; water lilies blooming yellow; frogs bulling. The lake surface was alive with water striders, larvae hatching, fish jumping, and sun sparkling. In the evening, loon laughter echoed off the islands as Venus shone brightly with dim Mars not far away. *Doug Reed*

7/11   Hudson River Gorge, HRM 284-257: We exited from the Indian River, just below Indian Lake, into the Hudson River on a three day rafting float trip down through the Hudson River Gorge, past Blue Ledge pool, to North Creek. Along the way we caught about 45 small brown and rainbow trout, and smallmouth bass up to a foot long. The bigger trout, said to exist in the Gorge, eluded us. A one-mile bushwhack from the river brought us to a small pond where we caught a few brook trout. Our guides cooked them up for us in three inches of bacon grease! The river water temperature ranged from 65°-70°F. *Jim Capossela. Toby McAfee, Bob Walters, Kathy McCarthy*

7/12 North Germantown, HRM 109: We hauled our seine across the warm, shallow tide flats through thick beds of wild celery of pondweed. We saw a glittering of silver in the back of the net and anticipated a nice haul of river herring. To our surprise the bag was filled with Atlantic menhaden, a marine herring, nearly five of them for every meter of bottom we had seined. These were young-of-the year, 19.0-38.0 mm in length. Although we could not taste any salt in the water, it was a good bet that their presence this far upriver was inspired by the drought-induced salty conditions sixty miles downriver. While taking a breather, we spotted a juvenile bald eagle flying low across the river, east to west, toward Inbocht Bay. This may have been a new summer fledgling. *Bob Schmidt, Tom Lake*

Nutten Hook, HRM 124: An hour later and 15 miles upriver we were still finding *yoy* Atlantic menhaden in our seine. We had never, in twenty years of sampling the river, encountered these marine herring this far upriver. They were less abundant here, only about one menhaden per meter seined. Their size was the same, 19.0-38.0 mm. *Bob Schmidt, Tom Lake*

Waterford, HRM 158: We were hauling our seine in the Mohawk River just west of Cohoes Falls looking for this year's crop of blueback herring. We found them by the score, mixed in with two species of fish that we rarely see in the Hudson River just a few miles away: spotfin shiners and logperch. While the Mohawk is the Hudson River's largest tributary, it still retains a somewhat different community of fishes. The water was 77°F. *Bob Schmidt, Tom Lake*

Adult **blueback herring**, by the millions, migrate in from the sea in April and May. In the first 150 miles of tidewater they adjust from salt water to freshwater. Then they navigate their way through several locks from the federal dam at Troy to the Erie Canal at Waterford, finally reaching the Mohawk River to spawn.

7/17   Esopus Meadows, HRM 87: Passengers aboard the tour boat *Teal* reportedly saw three harbor porpoises rolling in the Hudson River. The extended upriver range of menhaden this summer may be a lure. *Eric Kiviat*

Poughkeepsie, HRM 68: A record air temperature of 100°F was recorded today replacing the old record for the date of 98° set in 1991. *National Weather Service*

7/18 Poughkeepsie, HRM 74: In the oppressive 99°F heat and humidity, we heard the first katydids of summer. How fitting, yet, given the type of summer, not surprising. *John Mylod, Mary Brockway*

7/20 Athens, HRM 118: As I canoed north along the river, preparing to land at the put-in beneath the power lines, the head of a northern water snake was visible along the rocky shoreline. I managed to get close enough to see the body beneath the water as it quickly swam out of reach. I guessed it to be at least 18" long. *Gail Mihocko*

7/21 Athens, HRM 118: In the West Flats marsh I saw what I thought was a tern because of its dainty, flitting flight. The leading edges of its primaries were white with a black trailing edge. Upon landing on the exposed sand, a close inspection revealed a black head and bill, and orange legs. It was an adult Bonaparte's gull, keeping company with two adult ring-billed gulls. Later, I was "canoeing" through the mud at low tide after a long, mucky day in the marsh when I spotted a least bittern. It flew back and forth from the mud flats to the cattails. Less than twenty feet from the canoe the bittern began fishing in the tide pools and puddles that were splashing with killifish. The pickings were easy and, although I regret not having counted, the bittern must have gorged on at least thirty of these three-inch fish before I decided to move on. *Gail Mihocko*

Least bittern In three of the last four years (1996,1997,1999) I worked in twenty different marshes between Schodack (HRM 139) and Manitou (HRM 46). This summer I saw many more least bitterns than in either of the other two years. In addition to being somewhat uncommon, they are very secretive. *Gail Mihocko*

7/22   North Germantown, HRM 109: We seined in the rising tide looking for *yoy* river herring. This must have been a special time or tide for the net continually filled with clouds of baby striped bass, blueback herring, alewives, American shad, and spottail shiners. In the back of the net (it stuck me in the thumb!) was a feisty little two-inch white catfish. Water temperature was 79°F. *Tom Lake, Phyllis Lake*

Catfish can hurt! The first ray of their dorsal and pectoral fins are sharp. These are not spines, as with a striped bass or yellow perch, but a hardened ray, like those in a carp's dorsal fin. Much care must be taken when handling catfish to avoid getting "stuck."

River herring   by Tom Lake

   Nutten Hook, HRM 124: The three of us were standing there in knee-deep water, heads down, looking into the bag of our seine, shaking our heads at the incredible numbers of *yoy* American shad we had caught. Out in the narrow passage between Nutten Hook and Coxsackie a huge freighter, the *Sea Luck*, sped past heading south. It sent a six-foot wall of water ashore that wiped us out, carrying fish, seines, camera, sandals, sneakers and us many yards above the tideline. We survived, which was more than could be said of the camera. *Karin Limburg, Dennis Swaney, Tom Lake*

7/23   Croton Point, HRM 35: The warm shallows were a very toasty 83°F, and a salty 8.5 ppt. We could see many large and graceful

adult blue crabs scurrying across the sandy bottom. As we opened our seine, after a short haul across some open water, we found what looked like a shiny silver dollar nestled in a fold. Except that it was a fish, a spot (98 mm), a saltwater member of the drum family, and an uncommon visitor. We released many *yoy* American shad (60 mm), alewives (58 mm) and a few menhaden (63 mm). *Tom Lake, Christopher Letts*

Spot are a sporadic visitor to the Hudson estuary. Their colloquial name, "Lafayette," honors the *Marquis de Lafayette,* whose visit to New York City in 1824 coincided with unusually large numbers of these small drum in New York Harbor and the lower Hudson estuary. *Lafayette* was invited back to America to be honored for his role in the American Revolution on behalf of the American Colonies.

7/25   New York Harbor, Lower Bay: As part of the New York City Department of Environmental Protection's Floatables Study to reduce trash in New York Harbor, we noted the significant amount of angler trash left on the jetty at Midland Beach. A sponge crab, a female blue crab carrying eggs, was resting in the warm shallows on the incoming tide. *Christopher Scarcella*

"Sponge crab" is a description of a female blue crab carrying eggs. The eggs are carried under their tail which forms an apron on their abdomen. As the eggs mature, their color changes from black to orange. Just prior to hatching, the females blue crab appears to be carrying a "sponge" on her abdomen.

   Fishkill Creek, HRM 60: At the inlet to the Hudson, water visibility was unusually clear, greater than two feet. At the top of the flood, with the exception of a narrow outlet channel from Fishkill Creek, the bay at Denning Point was completely covered with water chestnut. I could hear and see large carp poking their snouts through the thick mat. Several green herons were foraging on top of the water chestnut and, in the cattails upstream, I could hear marsh wrens. I made some casts and caught a dozen 4"-6" white perch; this spring's crop of striped bass, none more than two inches long, also followed the lure. One of the creek's outlet stream, Melzingah Brook was dry. Its source, Melzingah Reservoir, was 22' below full. *Stephen Seymour*

7/26   Croton River, HRM 34: Standing by the railroad bridge at 5:30 AM, I took the time to watch a splendid sunrise over the Croton River marsh and gorge. As soon as there was enough light to see, hundreds of swallows of several species, but mostly tree swallows, swirled up into the sky to begin foraging: a veritable cloud of birds. An eagle came right down the middle of the Croton River and passed through the swallows seemingly without bothering them. As it flew over Croton Bay enough light was available to show the white tail feathers of a mature bird. *Christopher Letts*

7/29   Croton Bay, HRM 34: A low tide and vivid sunrise set the stage for a great blue heron ballet on a sandbar 200 yards off the railroad bridge. For about ten minutes I watched them fishing and vying for position on the sandbar. The ballet turned into a rhumba as an adult bald eagle swept down the Croton River, out across the bay, and banked for a landing on the bar. The gulls and herons gave the eagle plenty of room, but none flew, and the dance resumed. *Christopher Letts*

7/30   Croton Point, HRM 34.5: I labored up the landfill in the steamy air at 6:30 AM, spotted a Lapland longspur, and then was rewarded by the sight of an adult bald eagle flying the length of the Point to disappear toward the western shore. It continued to be very hot; everything was parched. This would be the tenth day in a row of 90°F air temperatures. *Christopher Letts*

Hook Mountain to George's Island, HRM 31-39: The river was flat as we headed north, the morning haze burned off. Our fishing line off Hook Mountain brought up oyster shells from ancient beds and small half-inch mud crabs. At Rockland Light we counted 21 cormorants and a dozen herring gulls. By evening we reached George's Island and spotted

a northern harrier. The next morning, on our return trip, a white catfish motored along on the surface as if to say, "Am not a bottom feeder!" *Daniel Wolff, Lorenzo Wolff*

Great blue heron   by Esther Kiviat

Staten Island, New York Harbor: After ushering out our guests from a 6:00-9:00 PM sail aboard the *Clearwater*, I returned to find three of the crew transfixed by some action in the water below the dock. They were watching a school of silverside gather in the light of the dock. From the shadows four or five striped bass would emerge circling and tightly herding the school, occasionally snapping for a meal. Soon, more fish began to arrive. I could not resist working the scene with a dip net. It was near midnight before we stopped, having caught some young northern stargazers, a few pipefish, and an Atlantic needlefish. The stargazers and needlefish were new experiences for me. *Sean Madden*

7/31 Croton Point, HRM 34.5: This was the driest July and the single hottest month on record. The desiccated landscape shows the strain. Lawns are baked, vines and bushes are dropping leaves, trees are dying. Streambeds are dry, pond and lake levels down, both wild and cultivated crops are failing. On Croton Point the landfill is the gold of a wheat field ready for harvest and the park smells like a haymow—hay cured on the stem. The land aches for rain. *Christopher Letts*

Mid-Hudson Valley: How hot was this July? It was the Hudson Valley's warmest in 104 years. The average daily temperature was 77°F, nearly 6½° warmer than the 104-year average. There were more 90+° days (17) than in any previous July. *John Thompson, Mohonk Lake Cooperative Weather Station*

Hudson Valley: Our spring bald eagle fledgling results showed that all five immature Hudson River bald eagles fledged successfully this summer. *Peter Nye, Craig Thompson*

Bald eagle fledges from tidewater nests:

1997	1998	1999
1	4	5

Bald eagle breeding pairs in Hudson tidewater

1992 -1995	1996	1997	1998	1999
1 per year	2	2	3	4*

* Five nesting pairs produced four young.

August 1999

It was kind of solemn, drifting down the big still river,
laying on our backs looking up at the stars...
Mark Twain, *Adventures of Huckleberry Finn*

8/1   Tenafly, NJ, HRM 17: There was a pied-billed grebe bobbing on the river and a dark-phase tiger swallowtail fluttered past. The most compelling observation, however, was the air temperature: 97°F. *Nancy Slowik*

   Manhattan, HRM 1: A juvenile scrawled cowfish (19 mm) was taken by *Cathy Drew* of The River Project in a small mesh minnow trap at Pier 26 in NYC. This tiny fish was the size and shape of a pea. *Bob Schmidt* identified it as a new species for the Hudson River. After some further analysis, it became obvious to us that this was an undescribed life stage of this fish. *Tom Lake*

8/2 Croton Point, HRM 34: A nice long low tide walk in the marsh to visit the fiddler crabs is a favorite August pastime. The rose mallows flaunt their huge blooms, herons and egrets stalk the tide flats, and big carp surge out of the water every minute or so. The fiddlers wave their claws in my direction and I wave back. I teased a pair of marsh wrens to within six feet of me and enjoyed the song of the male. Later, back in the park, I heard the song of a house wren, and then a Carolina wren farther up the hill singing, *"Teakettle, Teakettle."* How many places can one hear three species of wren in the space of 200 yards and five minutes? This was one more example of the biodiversity value of this peninsula in the estuary. *Christopher Letts*

8/3   Upper Nyack, HRM 30: A front came through so the weather was bearable but still no rain. The land was so parched that the lawns of the big riverfront homes appeared as though someone substituted an acre or two of yellow sand. *Lorenzo Wolff* and I turned over rocks on the mud flat looking for blue crabs, no larger than a thumbnail, for his aquarium. As his nine-year-old body bent over tide pools in search of prey, fifty yards away an immature black-crowned night heron did the same. He's the one with the yellow-green legs. *Daniel Wolff*

   Sleepy Hollow, HRM 28.5: Our NYSDEC striped bass survey crew seines beaches along the tidal Hudson each summer, from mid-July through mid-November, to sample for young-of-the-year and year class strength. Today, with our 200' net, we captured a pair of uncommon fish, juvenile northern stargazers. Each was less than two inches long with a yellow stripe and eyes on top of their head. *Ron Gelardi, Kim McKown, Matt Graff, Susan Olsen*

Tiger swallowtail butterfly   by Wayne Kocher

   Sleepy Hollow, HRM 28: We seined the beach at Kingsland Point Park, just below where the NYSDEC crew was working, and found an interesting mix of saltwater, brackish water, and freshwater fishes. Of the brackish water fish, by far the largest number was Atlantic silverside.

Down from freshwater were several dozen *yoy* striped bass and a surprise largemouth bass. In from the sea were seven *yoy* bluefish. *Christopher Letts, Mary Chalaney*

8/4   Garrison, HRM 52: It was hot, sunny, and dry. We went to Constitution Marsh hoping for some relief. As we approached the phragmites on the shore, a least bittern burst out of the reeds on wide, short wings. Its long yellow legs dangled down. From the bench on the boardwalk we could see smoke from the wildfire on Crow's Nest across the river. A helicopter, with a huge, dangling red bucket, brought river water to the blaze. Ruby-throated hummingbirds zipped along the marsh mallows and jewelweed and two kingfishers had a rattling argument over fishing territory. *Michael Shiffer, Elijah Shiffer, Amy Silberkleit, Isis Shiffer*

Croton Point, HRM 35: In the warm, salty shallows of Croton Point we caught two pinfish. There were also two scup in the net, known colloquially as a "porgy." Yesterday we captured scup ten miles downriver at Irvington as well. *Kim McKown, Matt Graff, Tom Hurst*

Pinfish and porgies (scup) are members of the saltwater porgy family. Like many other marine strays, they occur primarily as juveniles in the Hudson estuary.

Ossining, HRM 33: *Mary Chalaney* and I were seining for blue crabs for a Hudson River Foundation growth study. As we spread the seine, I noted a large and freshly dead white perch, minus one eye, on the beach. As I sorted through the contents of the net a few minutes later, I saw a fleshy white sphere about 10 mm in diameter. I picked it up, expecting that it was the missing perch eye, and found myself holding a juvenile northern puffer, a most unusual fish in the waters off Ossining. *Christopher Letts*

Puffers are always fun to find in your net. They are an ocean species, and the ones we catch in the estuary are nearly always small juveniles. Puffers have an amazing defense strategy; when threatened or agitated, they "inflate" themselves with air or water increasing their size to dissuade predators from swallowing them. Their colloquial name is "blowfish." Adult "puffed" puffers take on the proportions of a football. The juveniles we catch in the Hudson resemble ping-pong balls.

West Shokan, HRM 92: There had been no appreciable rain for over a month; a sweet birch had dried up on the west side of the house. At noon a young black bear, 3'-4' long, passed through the back yard from west to east, waving its nose in the air, turned around, and went back toward the west. At 6:00 PM, a four-point stag lay down to rest in the front yard. *John Bierhorst*

Bear Mountain, HRM 46: From the top of Perkins Memorial it seemed that fully half of Dunderberg Mountain was on fire. The rising smoke plumes were dense enough to cast a shadow on the Hudson River. The call of a nearby raven seemed almost a commentary on the somber scene. *Christopher Letts*

Tenafly, NJ, HRM 17: A drought emergency was declared for New Jersey. *Nancy Slowik*

8/6   Town of Esopus, HRM 88: *Dick Nelson* was fishing a plastic worm in the shallows just above Esopus Meadows when he hooked and landed a pacu. This pacu was new to the river and became species number 208. *Robert Daniels*

Pacu, a freshwater fish from South America' Amazon drainage, is related to piranhas (same subfamily). They are a popular tank fish for fish hobbyists. They are sometimes released into area waters when the thrill of taking care of them is gone. At least one other pacu is known from the watershed (250 mm, 270 gms.) caught July 28, 1994, in the Mohawk River.

Croton River, HRM 34: We had a spectacular sunrise. Yesterday there were no kestrels on the peninsula; this morning a dozen flew past, two weeks earlier than last year. Marsh hawks, seen singly for months, could now be viewed 4-5 at a time. At 6:00 AM the scene was lively. Schools of snapper bluefish were driving baitfish right to the waterline, and there to receive them was a chorus of long-legged wading birds. From one spot I counted twenty great blue herons and five great egrets. The question of what they were all dining on was partially answered with several throws of a cast net. Silverside were present, and tiny striped bass, but the bulk of the catch was jewel-like, glistening menhaden about two inches long. *Christopher Letts, Midgie Taube*

8/7   Lower Hudson Valley: Summer 1999 was declared to be the worst drought in 105 years for the lower Northeast. *U.S. Department of Commerce*

Coeymans Elementary School seining
by Fran Martino

Peekskill, HRM 43: The drought continued. Salinity was above 7.0 ppt (more than 20% of seawater at this latitude), nearly twice what would be expected for Peekskill in August. Across the river Dunderberg Mountain remained aflame, as it had been for nearly a week. The stands of hardwoods on the mountain behind Jones Point are a winter roosting area for bald eagles. Will they find the spot as desirable this winter? By day smoke obscured the river; by night the mountain glowed with angry red patches. *Tom Lake, Earl Harkins*

Garrison, HRM 52: The waterfall on Indian Brook was a ghost of its usual flow. A Louisiana waterthrush, a small warbler, was walking up the wet rocks by the waterfall. Its legs were worm pink. The bird was in constant motion, devouring bugs and worms it found in

the mud, on logs, in the moss and on rocks. Tail bobbing, head down, body horizontal, it ignored our presence, absorbed in its feeding. *Amy Silberkleit, Michael Shiffer, Elijah Shiffer, Isis Shiffer*

8/8   Garrison, HRM 52: We went out in Constitution Marsh to collect mud for the biological monitoring of the Foundry Cove Superfund Remediation. To our delight, we were treated to an incredible diversity of birds. Raptors: peregrine falcon, American kestrel, northern harrier, turkey vulture; Waterfowl: green-winged teal, wood duck, mallard; Wading birds: great blue heron, green heron, great egret; Shore birds: least sandpiper, greater yellowlegs, killdeer. That was only the tip of the iceberg, so to speak, for there were shoals of menhaden being herded by snapper bluefish and needlefish, plying the water's surface like miniature submarines. Just another day in the marsh. *Eric Lind, Rich Anderson*

8/9   East Greenwich, HRM 188: I got hooked today on the Battenkill. For years I have tested its relatively pristine water, swam in and paddled down this beautiful river, and sat on super survey committees, all on a mission to "preserve and enhance" the Battenkill. But today was my best firsthand experience about the most significant social issue confronting the Battenkill—community, recreational conflict. Basically, we can't get along using the river in increasing numbers for a variety of recreational activities, simultaneously. On this hot August evening I went for a dip in the East Greenwich village swimming hole, eleven miles up the Battenkill from the Hudson. I had not talked to my neighbor, *Russell Anderson*, for years, but I called out my presence as I approached. He was fly fishing for trout, backcasting with a practically invisible monofilament leader that was suddenly wrapped , and then broken off, around my head. I yelled again that I was behind him. Startled, he turned, waved, and then went back to fishing, tying on a new leader. I sat down to put my shoes on and get the fishing line out of my hair when I realized that I had a finely barbed hook buried in my temple. "Uh, Russell,

I'm going to need your help!" He worked with his pliers for 15 minutes—apologetically and gingerly—and finally removed a perfect size 12 blue-winged olive dry fly from my head. I have it mounted on my wall (the dry fly). I guess we all need to communicate more than every few years. *Doug Reed*

8/11   New Hamburg, HRM 67.5: At sunrise a light cloud cover obscured the eastern horizon depriving us of a view of a partial solar eclipse. To river life it appeared that dawn was simply slow to arrive. With my binoculars I could see 15 miles downriver into the Highlands and wisps of white smoke from the fires that yet raged. *Tom Lake*

Croton Point, HRM 34.5: I spotted a yellow-breasted chat in the fencerow between the Croton-Harmon railroad yard and the athletic field. It was in the mesh fence with an English sparrow right beneath it for size reference. I had been seeing many mockingbirds there, and there were several in the fencerow as well. But the chat wasn't big enough for a mockingbird. I actually said to myself, "What kind of mockingbird are you?" Then it clicked. This was the first of this species I had ever seen at Croton Point. *Christopher Letts*

8/12   North Germantown, HRM 109: We were there to catch fish but we had to appreciate the majesty of an immature bald eagle as it flew up the river toward us, then flared off to the west toward Inbocht Bay. We seined at the boat ramp, between launchings of pleasure craft. The activity did not seem to bother the fish. We caught a dozen *yoy* smallmouth bass as well as our target fish, *yoy* blueback herring, mixed in with American shad and alewives. In the hour we seined I counted no fewer than a dozen tiger swallowtails drifting by. I have seen more of them this year in migration than ever before. Water temperature was 78°F. *Tom Lake, Bob Schmidt, Alec Schmidt, Phyllis Lake*

8/13   Copake, HRM 106: I had my Bard College graduate ichthyology class seining along the Roeliff Jansen Kill just below its

origin at Robinson's Pond near Copake. I use this spot as an example of how impoundments change the fish fauna of streams. Among the usual array of largemouth bass, pumpkinseed sunfish, and golden shiners, we saw a flash of red fins. It turned out to be a four-inch rudd. Robinson Pond is the only reproducing population in the Northeast for this introduced species of minnow. *Bob Schmidt* (See Vol. IV, pp 29-30.)

Mine Point, HRM 74: The river was a warm 80°F. Overhead four turkey vultures and one red-tailed hawk vied for air space, soaring on the afternoon thermals. One of the vultures strayed into the redtail's space. The redtail flipped over, showed some talons, and the vultures moved off. I found 6½ dozen "keeper" blue crabs in my pots—very few throwbacks. This is going to be a good season. *John Mylod*

Blue crab size (carapace width) terminology
Jumbos are the biggest and the best of the catch—the prime market crab (7"+).
#1 Jimmy are the next largest crab and most commonly caught size (6"+).
#2 are smaller crabs but marketable, the minimum market size (5-5½").
Throwbacks are < 5".

Town of Wappinger, HRM 67: We lost a friend today, our harbinger of spring. Our 20-year-old shadbush had dropped all its leaves earlier in the summer in an effort to survive. But today it became apparent that the tree had succumb to the drought. We had trickled water continually to its roots for days with no success. *Tom Lake, Phyllis Lake*

Croton Point, HRM 35: As our beach seine came ashore it was a solid wall of juvenile jellyfish. They were small, fingernail size, moon jellyfish. These are true jellyfish and not the more common comb jellies (ctenophores). *Tom Lake, Brenda Freeman-Bates, Rebecca Schavrien, Karen Martis*

Bay Ridge Flats, Upper Bay, New York Harbor: A ten minute trawl on the Bay Ridge Flats brought to the tanks aboard the Hudson

River sloop *Clearwater* an amazing display of form and function—two pipefish, no more than three inches long, a northern puffer, fully "puffed," and a lined sea horse with its prehensile tail entwined in a cluster of sponge. For those on board the catch served as testimony to the rich diversity of New York Harbor. *Sean Madden*

Black-crowned night heron   by Wayne Kocher

8/14   Mid-Hudson Valley: In twenty-four hours, up to three inches of rain fell in the Mid-Hudson Valley Region bringing relief to flora and fauna alike. *Tom Lake*

   Croton River, HRM 34: It was dawn at the Croton trestle at the mouth of the Croton River. There were 25 great blue heron and great egrets lined up along the bay like customers waiting for their morning coffee and buttered bagel. *Christopher Letts*

   Alpine, NJ, HRM 18: The Hudson River sloop *Clearwater* shared the dock with a black-crowned night heron on a beautiful Palisades evening. Six of us sat on deck and watched as the heron methodically stepped its way along

the narrow dock railing. The bird was one of three we saw circling earlier, silhouetted in the fading light over the Palisades. It had been a great day for augury; we had kingfishers, a great blue heron, and an osprey cross our bow. *Sean Madden*

8/15   Croton Point, HRM 35: The sun had set behind Hi Tor and our lanterns now lit up the broad expanse of beach as we set our 200' haul seine. Just a few hours before scores of swimmers had filled the beach and the sandy shallows. With the onset of darkness they were gone, to be replaced by...? Thirty of us were gathered on the beach to find out. As we hauled the net back onto the sand, it glistened with dozens of striped bass, white perch, Atlantic menhaden, and two of the predators of the night: bluefish and Atlantic needlefish. Water temperature was 79°F; salinity was 11.4 ppt. *Lloyd Ellman, Fred Ellman, Christopher Letts, Phyllis Lake, Tom Lake*

8/16   Nyack, HRM 28: The Tappan Zee had a late afternoon summer haze, the air was salty, and the river was flat as glass. On our way to pick some strings of crab pots we noticed a surface disturbance some distance ahead of our boat. As we neared, we could see two harbor seals and they appeared to be playing on the surface. They may have had some fish. Moving on to our seventy pots, we found that we had caught nearly six bushels of blue crabs. The water temperature was 81°F; salinity was 12.8 ppt. *Paul Stanton, Robert Gabrielson*

8/17   West Shokan, HRM 92: A new and sizeable occurrence of the rare woods-rush—233 fruiting stems—turned up at elevation 740'. Five other rushes were noted in the same spot: soft rush, path rush, grass-leaved rush, narrow-leaved rush, and sharp-fruited rush. Despite the severe 1999 drought the springs at this site were still running. *John Bierhorst*

   Town of Esopus, HRM 87: As we walked our dog this evening we had a great surprise. It was a nighthawk flight day (dusk). In 15 minutes we saw more than fifty nighthawks, and then it got too dark to see them. *Fran Drakert, Bill Drakert*

Osprey carrying menhaden   by Wayne Kocher

Croton Point, HRM 35: During a morning low tide on the beach, I was talking to some *Pace University* students about the workings of the estuary. We looked up to see an osprey pass close overhead heading west, out to the river. I commented that even though bald eagles had great spiritual importance to Native Americans, osprey were held in similar high esteem as consummate fishers. Less than five minutes later, as we began to haul a seine through the wild celery beds, the osprey came back from the river. It passed close overhead, as if showing off its prize, with a large menhaden in its talons. In the seine were three pairs of "doublers," mated blue crabs. With much care, we eased them back into the bed of wild celery from which they had come. The river was 81°F; salinity was 9.6 ppt. After the program, as we were leaving, we spotted a marsh hawk, with its bright white rump patch, hunting on the landfill. Over the landfill, a pair of osprey soared, their circles intersecting. *Tom Lake, Christopher Letts, Chris Bowser, Judy Chamberlain*

Most of the **osprey** in the Hudson Valley are travelers, migrating from wintering areas far to the south, to northern breeding areas along the Great Lakes and coastal New England. Female osprey begin to migrate back south in July, males begin in August. Most have left by late September. They will fly south, covering as much as 235 miles a day to wintering locations as far south as Brazil, Venezuela, and Columbia, in South America. This journey may total 4500-5800 miles. *Pete Nye*

"Doubler" is an appropriate description of mated blue crabs. When a female is ready to mate, she releases a "perfume" (pheromone) into the water to attract male crabs. Once she selects a male, she will make her final moult and become a softshell crab. The male then cradles the female in his walking legs and they mate. She will not become "pregnant" right away; instead, the male gives the female sperm packages which she will store until the time is right for her to fertilize her eggs. Having consummated their union, the male will continue to cradle the female (as a doubler) until her new shell hardens and she is no longer as vulnerable. This may take 24-36 hours, depending upon water temperature.

Sandy Hook, NJ: There has been an enormous run of three-inch *yoy* menhaden this summer; fishermen call them "peanut bunker." Today we had a fluke blitz (summer flounder) at the tip of Sandy Hook, chasing bunker up to the surface and even jumping clear of the water as they were feeding. One angler had caught and released eighty fluke in the 14" range, using foul-hooked peanut bunker as bait. I called around and it appeared that peanut bunker were thick along the shore from Cape Cod to Chesapeake Bay. *Dery Bennett*

8/18 Hudson North Bay, HRM 119: The overactive, animated marsh wren is one of my favorite birds to watch. They are very bold and territorial and are not inhibited in speaking their mind when one ventures into their territory. On this day I watched two adults frantically feeding at least four young (still with yellow gapes and downy head tufts). Their constant scolding and chattering sounds probably keep them in touch with each other while at the same time alerted each other to my presence. While I stood still, they often came within four feet of me where I could clearly see them feeding, picking spiders and insects from pickerelweed and wild rice. *Gail Mihocko*

8/19   Garrison, HRM 52: It was a daybreak to remember at Constitution Marsh. As the sun rose, the clouds went from rose mallow pink to oriole orange to goldenrod yellow, and then brightened to egret white. *Eric Lind*

8/20   Stockport Flats to Middleground Flats, HRM 120-117: For three hours on a drizzly, calm afternoon at low tide, we led a canoe trip for the Columbia County Land Conservancy south along the shore of the estuary. Canoes ranged from an old Coleman to a handcrafted cedar and mahogany to an Old Town built in 1933 to a new and sophisticated Kevlar *We-no-nah*. In our travels we spotted 5 bald eagles (3 immature, 2 adults), snowy egrets, great blue herons, black ducks, cormorants, kingfishers, muskrats and hummingbirds. Twenty-five years ago, if someone said "estuary," the reply would have been "Bless you!" *Fran Martino, Kevin Oldenberg*

8/22   South Nyack, HRM 26: On this Sunday morning a softball game stopped dead in the fourth inning as all the players looked up to see an osprey flying from right field toward third base carrying a big silver fish in its talons. *Daniel Wolff*

Sleepy Hollow, HRM 28: While more than a hundred onlookers watched from the beach we hauled our seine across a stretch of shallow, sandy, river bottom. With no vegetation we expected our catch would be pelagic fish, those likely to be in open, unprotected water, built for speed rather than concealment. Dozens of five-inch bluefish flopped in the folds of our net alongside an equal number of their prey, Atlantic silverside. One markedly different fish was nestled in the bottom of the net: an inshore lizardfish (154 mm). This predator had been lying in wait on the bottom, blending perfectly with the tan and tawny brown of the sand. Water 78°F; salinity was 11.6 ppt. *Christopher Letts, Tom Lake*

8/23   Rondout Creek, HRM 92: It was only a little over an hour before low tide and in the clear shallows of the marsh at Kingston Point, I spotted a pair of mating blue crabs. The male was on top, cradling the female, and I was able to carefully measure him without disturbing their courtship. His carapace width was 6½". *Gail Mihocko*

Hillsdale Park and Recreation Summer Program
by Fran Martino

Kingston Point, HRM 92: Ruby-throated hummingbirds were in abundance on this sunny and hot day, presumably feeding in preparation of the long migration soon to come. All day I saw them out of the corner of my eye buzzing around the marsh visiting jewelweed (spotted touch-me-not) and purple loosestrife. *Gail Mihocko*

Croton Point, HRM 34.5: The athletic field was covered with shorebirds this morning and the air was filled with their cries. Greater yellowlegs, more than one hundred mixed "peeps" (sandpipers), and about fifty Wilson's plovers and killdeer, fed, flew, and rested. *Christopher Letts*

38

8/24 Croton Point, HRM 34.5: I heard a red-breasted nuthatch today at Croton Point. What was that bird doing there in August? Tiny tin horns! The wild cherries were ripe and the birds were working them over: Orioles, jays, woodpeckers. There was a huge flock of *yoy* cowbirds, a juvenile bobolink, a pair of greater yellowlegs, eight great egrets, and a half dozen osprey. One was carrying a catfish. *Christopher Letts*

8/25 Waterford, HRM 158: We were seining along the shore in the backwaters of the Erie Canal's Lock 3. This reach of the Mohawk River continually surprises us with a community of fishes that differs significantly from the Hudson River only a few miles away. On our final haul of the day we had yet another surprise, a brindled madtom (31 mm). *C.L. Smith* (1985:90) lists the easternmost record of this little catfish as Lock 7 on the Erie Canal; this specimen, from Lock 3, was a slight range extension. *Bob Schmidt, Alec Schmidt, Christopher Letts, Tom Lake*

Have you ever wondered where **fish names** come from? Naked goby. Fat sleeper. Speckled worm eel. Northern stargazer. Foureye butterflyfish. Hogchoker. The Names of Fishes Committee of the American Fisheries Society is the recognized authority on fish names, both naming fishes and changing their names. In recent years they have been considering making changes for some North American fish names that have been perceived as offensive or inappropriate, *e.g.,* jewfish and squawfish. While they're at it, I'd like them to think about renaming those 24 species of catfish known as **madtoms** (more than 60% of all North American catfishes are known as madtoms). I personally find "madtom" to be insulting. How about something like "congenialtoms?" *Tom "Not Madtom" Lake*

Nutten Hook, HRM 124: The container ship *Mars World* surged past heading downriver. The wake from the vessel was enormous. As it approached the beach, all of the water was sucked away in a strong undertow. Seconds later the five-foot-high roller crashed ashore as a brown, muddy, viscous, wave. As it retreated, scores of *yoy* striped bass, alewife,

blueback herring, and American shad were left flopping above the reach of the tide where they had been tossed by the crest of the wave. Among them was an eleven-inch black crappie. We watched and waited for the rebound of the wake. It came back ashore six times, at several minute intervals, having bounced off the opposite shore less than a half-mile away. *Bob Schmidt, Alec Schmidt, Christopher Letts, Tom Lake*

Spanish mackerel   by Tom Lake

Nyack, HRM 27: *Bob Gabrielson* found a surprise when he went out to pick his "bunker nets" to get some bait for his crab pots. Caught in the mesh of his gillnet were two Spanish mackerel—two large Spanish mackerel! Each was 25" in length and weighed 4 pounds. The salinity was 12.8 ppt and the water temperature was 78°F.

While **Spanish mackerel** are a rather rare summer visitor to the estuary, a few seem to show up each summer. They are occasionally taken in crab pots and by sport fishermen in the lower Hudson. Although they can grow to three feet in length, a typical Hudson River Spanish mackerel is 10"-20" long. The much more common mackerel of the lower Hudson estuary and New York Bight is the Atlantic mackerel.

8/26 Edgewater, NJ, HRM 7: *Ron Ingold* runs a line of crab pots near the old Edgewater ferry terminal about four miles south of the George Washington Bridge. When he pulled his pots today, he found two rock crabs inside. Both were males (33 mm, 127 mm. The largest one weighed over a pound.

Rock crabs are a common saltwater crustacean of New England and the New York Bight. While not common in the Hudson River, these were found not far from New York Harbor's Upper Bay. Their presence in the lower estuary was likely related to the drought and increased salinity of the lower Hudson. These are "true crabs," because they have four pairs of walking legs and one pair of claws. Swimming crabs, like the blue crab and lady crab, have three pairs of walking legs, a pair of claws, and one modified pair of "swimming paddles."

8/27 Garrison, HRM 51: One of the benefits of a chicken dinner aboard the Hudson River sloop *Clearwater* is the inevitable presence of bones and scraps that serve as near irresistible bait for our eel pot. When I raised the trap this morning, I found a curious little, muddy, two-inch-long fish between two wriggling eels. In our tank the fish spent most of its time hiding on the bottom but once it alighted on the glass side, the fused pelvic fins, that form a sucker disc, quickly helped me identify it as a naked goby—a first for me. In drought summers, this fish has been found as far upriver as Danskammer Point (HRM 66.5). *Sean Madden*

8/28 Garrison, HRM 51: After a short trawl just offshore of the Garrison Boat Club mooring field, we hauled the otter trawl aboard the *Clearwater* with its cod end swollen, practically bursting with life. When I released the knot that held the cod end a writhing, squiggling, glistening cascade poured forth into the catch tub. When they were all counted, we had 25 hogchokers, 5 white catfish, 5 juvenile weakfish, 2 white perch, 2 juvenile bluefish, 12 adult blue crabs, 15 juvenile blue crabs, a handful of bay anchovies, and an amazed group of spectators. *Sean Madden*

An **otter trawl** is a small mesh net pulled behind a vessel. They are designed to catch fish at different levels in the water column. Otter trawls can be of varying lengths and widths but all are held open as they are "fished" by the pressure of moving water against a pair of heavy doors; one door is set to port, one to starboard. The doors are usually made of wood with a lead foot (lower edge). Most trawls have a cod end, tied shut when fishing, opened wide to spill out the catch when brought aboard.

Tappan Zee, HRM 27: One of the intriguing aspects of fishing in the lower Hudson, with its proximity to the sea, is that you never know what you might catch. We were bottom fishing from our boat with worms when we caught a foot-long striped sea robin. We'd never seen one before in the river. The warm, salty water of summer probably brought this fish upriver. *Brian DiGirolamo, Sherry Piesco*

Tenafly, NJ, HRM 17: I was leading a 7:00 PM Greenbrook Sanctuary evening walk program to Patriot's Leap Vista. From there we spotted 18 common nighthawks migrating south over the Hudson. They appeared to be catching insects "on the wing" as they flew southward. *Nancy Slowik* (See Esopus Meadows, August 18.)

New York Harbor, Lower Bay: The tide was flooding in Prince's Bay; visibility in the bay was near five feet. I watched snapper blues chase schools of "peanut bunker" (small menhaden) and silversides into a frenzy. The schools of bait continually changed direction, flawlessly, in their effort to confuse the blues and escape. Blue crabs were scurrying along the bottom. *Jim Scarcella*

8/29 Esopus Island, HRM 85: *Lynn Falbella* was boating on the river when she spotted a harbor seal hauled out on a buoy near Esopus Island. The seal was about four-feet-long.

Poughkeepsie, HRM 74: There were 35 dozen keeper-crabs in my sixty pots. Only one in a hundred was female, and only one in a hundred females was mature. I tossed back another thirty dozen that were too small. The river temperature had dropped from 80°F to 77° in two weeks. *John Mylod*

Hudson River blue crabs are known for their yearly cycles of abundance and scarcity. Some of this fluctuation may be linked to the severity of winter and the subsequent mortality of wintering young-of-the-year. Blue crabs have interesting colloquial names known mostly to rivermen. On their abdomen, males have an apron the shape of a rocket ship (or the Washington Monument). The adult males are called "Jimmys." Immature females have a triangular apron and are called "Sallys." Mature females have a dome shaped apron and are called "Sookies."

Town of Poughkeepsie, HRM 73: The estuarine "salt front" (≥3.0 ppt), buoyed by high moon tides and the summer's drought, moved closer to the public water intake at Poughkeepsie. Consumption advisories were issued for those people who have severely restricted sodium intake diets. *Darren O'Sullivan*

Tivoli Bays

by Esther Kiviat

Autumn

September 1999

The Windhover
I CAUGHT this morning morning's minion,
kingdom of daylight's dauphin,
dapple-dawn-drawn Falcon,
in his riding of the rolling level
underneath him steady air, and striding
High there, how he rung upon the reign
of a wimpling wing In his ecstacy!
then off, off forth on swing...
Gerard Manley Hopkins

9/1   Poughkeepsie, HRM 74: I was dragging for my crab pot leadline when my drag hook became hung down on the bottom of the river. I could feel the enormous strength of the river's current. After much effort I managed to pull the "hang down" to the surface. It was an old crab pot filled with mud and silt that I had lost overboard three years ago when I had been out setting pots—a swell from a passing boat, a list, and a topple overboard. The pot was open, had not been baited, and therefore had not been functioning as a "ghost pot" for three years. I shook it out, cleaned it up, baited it, and dropped it back into the river, this time attached to a leadline. The rest of my pots had thirty dozen crabs, some to seven-inch carapace width. The water was 75°F. *John Mylod*

Ghost pots and **ghost nets** are a concern to all commercial fishermen. They result from lost gear, when an anchor net is torn from it mooring, a drift net becomes hung down on a fast and cannot be recovered, or a pot or trap breaks from its anchor line. All continue to fish, to some degree, long after they can be tended. Fish and crabs become caught and cannot escape. The term "ghost" refers to the fact that this gear looms insidiously on the bottom of the river prepared to capture and kill the unwary. While ghost gear in marine waters can fish for a considerable length of time, the strong currents of the Hudson estuary tend to bring nets to the bottom fairly

quickly rendering them relatively harmless. Traps and pots must wait until they rust to provide an escape. Ghost gear in the Hudson is not epidemic and most commercial fishermen go to extreme lengths to recover lost gear.

Garrison, HRM 51.5: What a show! I was walking along the *Jim Rod Memorial Boardwalk* at the Constitution Marsh Sanctuary when I spotted a school of *yoy* menhaden (at least fifty fish) with a school of *yoy* bluefish pursuing them from underneath. Bluefish chasing menhaden is not a typical Hudson Highlands summer event. Atlantic menhaden in the marsh is rather unusual and probably results from the summer drought. *Eric Lind*

9/4   Hyde Park, HRM 80: *Larry* and *Sheryl Lozier* were having their shallow backyard pond near the Fall Kill, 2½ miles east of the Hudson, deepened so that fish would survive the winter cold and ice. During the excavation, a few large bones and fragments of a tusk came up in the excavator's scoop. Archaeologists *Bob Funk* and *Chris Lindner* concluded that these were the bones of a long extinct animal, probably a mastodont or a mammoth. Teeth are the most diagnostic trait used in differentiating between the two animals, but no teeth had been found. The bones were very well preserved, having been sealed in an anaerobic marl layer about three feet below the bottom of the pond. One of the bones recovered was a humerus, or upper arm bone. It had a diameter of 12". When articulated with an ulna that was found, they were 67" (1.7 m) long. One anomalous bone was also recovered that was tentatively identified as belonging to an extinct form of giant bison *(Bison bison antiquus). Tom Lake*

The Lozier's backyard pond is actually a 0.13 acre **kettle hole**, spring fed, and 232' above the Hudson River. Kettle ponds, or kettle holes, result from a depression left in glacial drift (debris) made by the wasting away of a detached mass of ice that was either wholly or partly buried. Glacial drift is all of the material that the glacier had picked up and carried on its journey, from minute clay-sized particles to rocks the size of a school bus. When the block of ice melted, a pond was formed in the depression.

Hyde Park, HRM 80: Some excavation was done as the site was investigated through October. Little else was recovered. Many questions remained: Were these bones an isolated find? How old were the bones? Were these from a mammoth, a mastodont, or something else? Could this have been an elephant that ran away from a local circus a hundred years or more ago and drowned in the pond? The latter question was investigated. No one, it seems, had ever reported a missing elephant.

The site's suspected antiquity was verified by *Dave Strayer* of the Institute of Ecosystem Studies. He analyzed an assemblage of mollusks recovered from the clay in the bottom of the pond. He concluded that, to find this community of mollusks today, you would have to travel 1,200 miles north to the Hudson Bay drainage. The 12,000 year-old Pleistocene epoch of Dutchess County had moved considerably north.

The **Pleistocene** is only one of many geological time periods that scientists use to divide up the earth's history. These make comprehension of time depth and comparisons of time frames, easier. The Pleistocene began about two million years ago, corresponding to the advent of our genus, *Homo*, in Africa. The Pleistocene ended about 10,000 years

ago. We are currently living in what is called the Holocene epoch, or "recent time."

Hyde Park, HRM 80: The Paleontological Research Institution (PRI) and Cornell University's department of Geological Sciences, in Ithaca, NY, were contacted for assistance in locating the rest of the skeleton. As autumn turned to winter, the site was left with a promise to return in the spring to resume the search.

Note: See Afterword for a 2000 update

Monarch butterfly   by Wayne Kocher

9/4   Senasqua, HRM 36: As we drew our seine into the swash it teemed with hundreds of small *yoy* menhaden. However, something different was slipping in and out of view. We parted the bunker with our hands and found a small crevalle jack. *Eric Lind, Murray Fisher* (See *jacks* family of fishes, November 11.)

Tappan Zee, HRM 27: *Ian Raywid* and I were out in our Sea Ox at first light to pick the gillnet that we had set the night before: fresh bait for our blue crab pots. The river was gorgeous! In the ten minute run from the dock to the net we saw no fewer than a hundred schools of "bait" (Atlantic menhaden or bunker) breaking the river's surface, being chased by bluefish. In my sixty years on the Hudson River, I have *never* seen as much bait, as much life, as I have seen in the river this summer. Dozens of

15"-17" bunker were in the net as well as eight 17"-20" weakfish. The bigger weakies bounce off the small mesh. There may be some around the size they call "tiderunners," 10-12 pounders. Small summer flounder in numbers I have never seen in the Tappan Zee continue to show up in our crab pots. Larger, legal-size (14") summer flounder were being caught off the docks around Nyack. *Bob Gabrielson*

9/8   Ulster Park, HRM 88: Today was our last ruby-throated hummingbird sighting for the year. We often note the arrival of a species, but rarely the departure. *Fran Drakert, Bill Drakert*

Poughkeepsie-Highland, HRM 77.2-76.5: Despite recent rains and releases from Sacandaga Reservoir in the Adirondacks, the "salt front" had surpassed the public water intakes at Poughkeepsie and Highland and had reached river mile 78. *Darren O'Sullivan*

Salt front: A consumption advisory for people with severely restricted salt intake diets must be issued when salt (sodium) is greater than 20 milligrams per liter in public drinking water. At 250 milligrams per liter (2.5 ppt), the water begins to taste salty.

9/11   North Germantown, HRM 109: We hauled our seine for several hundred feet along the beach at North Germantown looking for *yoy* blueback herring, with almost no success. On a hunch we moved our net into the narrow slip of the boat launch, and immediately caught all we needed. Most were around 60 mm long. The water was 75°F. *Bob Schmidt, Alec Schmidt, Kathy Schmidt, Tom Lake*

New Hamburg, HRM 67.5: It was 390 years ago today that Henry Hudson and the *Half Moon* sailed past. What a different river that must have been. Henry and his crew would not have seen the giant carp flopping in the shallows, or watched the elegant mute swans paddle along the shore. The green herons and great blue herons of his time would have needed a different perch from which to fish than the ubiquitous mats of water chestnut that now choke the shallows. In our haste to shrink the

world we have certainly clouded our view of the past. *Tom Lake*

River of Words
The Hudson River is a beautiful scene,
As it lies in the valley with its own color scheme.
As the wind blows and puts ripples in the waves and trees,
The birds above migrate and follow the river with ease.
Layers of history are embedded in the river's bed,
As we learn about them in the pages, we have read.
Explored in 1609 by Henry Hudson in his ship the *Half Moon*,
We gather here to ponder our thoughts on this afternoon.
Amelia Dosio, New Windsor School, NY

Chelsea, HRM 65.2: It looked for all the world as though it were raining. But the midday sun was out and the sky was blue. The calm surface of the river, as far as I could see, was dimpled. Thousands, maybe hundreds of thousands of tiny dimples, each representing a two-inch *yoy* herring, dabbling on the surface for food, insect life, black ants. It seemed like an entire year-class of alewives, blueback herring, and American shad were slowly swimming south in the current, heading to sea. *Tom Lake*

9/12   Englewood, NJ, HRM 13.5: On a beautiful late summer day I let the last of the flood tide carry me in my canoe upriver. With the current doing the work, I sat back and watched a kettle of broad-winged hawks overhead. What a thrill. I counted several osprey fishing in the river and a red-tailed hawk soared over the Palisades. *Bob Rancan*

Manhattan, HRM 1: We captured a juvenile (80 mm) gag in our gear today from The River Project's Pier 26. This is a very rare fish species in the Hudson. Salinity was 25 ppt; water temperature was 70°F. *Cathy Drew*

Gag is the common name for a species of grouper, a member of the sea bass family of temperate and tropical marine fishes. The gag's normal range is from North Carolina to Florida to the Gulf of Mexico, but juveniles occasionally range northward as far as Massachusetts.

Chris Letts with blue crab   by Tom Lake

9/13   Town of Marbletown, HRM 92: A wood turtle, a species of "special concern" in New York State, was busily consuming a large mushroom 300' from the stream in Esopus Gorge. After an unusually severe summer drought the cataracts that ordinarily shoot from the walls of the gorge were completely dry. *John Bierhorst*

Croton Point, HRM 34-35: The bountiful Hudson seems to be more bountiful than ever this year. Talk at the docks and boat ramps is of seemingly unending schools of baitfish, mostly finger-sized menhaden. Ten minutes with a dip net in the wild celery yielded scores of small blue crabs and hundreds of shrimp, more than I had ever seen. The surface of Croton Bay was covered with gulls, osprey, and cormorants, and wading birds were present in large numbers to take advantage of the season's largess. I don't recall seeing so many gulls in one place since the garbage dump stopped rolling onto Croton

Point 15 years ago. Semipalmated plovers mixed with a large flock of killdeer on the athletic field. Jerking its way around a tiny grass puddle was a solitary sandpiper. Appropriately enough, it was alone. *Christopher Letts*

Tenafly, NJ, HRM 17: It was a flight day along the Palisades. An adult peregrine falcon flew past Patriot's Leap Vista. As the bird circled back, a resident red-tailed hawk flew out from its perch with talons extended. The peregrine decided to move along. A total of three peregrines passed by today as well as a sharp-shinned hawk, a Cooper's hawk, nine osprey, three broad-winged hawks, an American Kestrel, and forty monarch butterflies. *Nancy Slowik*

9/14   Nyack Beach State Park, HRM 31: Students from *Pearl River Middle School* were helping us sample the river life in the shadow of Hook Mountain. The NYSDEC Marine Division striped bass survey crew set their 200' seine, hoping to catch *yoy* striped bass. Their net came ashore and they had several thousand little striped bass, enough to keep the crew counting for a half hour. Something different in the net caught our eye—a silver saltwater fish called a spot (46 mm). And then there were the eels... The salinity was 9.5; water temperature was 75°F. *Christopher Letts, Regina Gelman, Frank Auriemna, Tom Lake*

Nyack Beach State Park, HRM 31: We had not been catching anything out of the ordinary all day and we were afraid we would not be able to show anything exciting to the students from *Pearl River Middle School*. We asked the river to give us something to excite the kids, and she provided. As the net came in, we had more than a dozen big, squirming eels. The students, reluctant at first, soon were reaching in and grabbing for the nearly frictionless critters. Some were over two-feet-long. *Ron Gelardi, Kim McKown, Matt Graff, Susan Olsen*

9/15   Poughkeepsie, HRM 75: In seventy pots, I caught forty dozen market-sized blue crabs. I tossed back twenty dozen more that were undersized. There were many small, dime-sized, *yoy* blue crabs clinging to the pots to get a free meal. That augurs well for next year. The water temperature was 74°F. *John Mylod*

Sandy Hook, NJ: The "peanut bunker," *yoy* menhaden, had been so thick here all summer that occasional strong waves would leave some flopping on the beach. Anglers had been reporting wall-to-wall menhaden in Sandy Hook and Raritan bays. Several times we have seen summer flounder come out of the water chasing them. *Pam Carlsen, Dery Bennett*

9/16 Chelsea, HRM 65.2: The storm surge from tropical storm *Floyd,* formerly a category four hurricane, moved up the Hudson. Low tide at midday was indistinguishable from a normal high tide—the tide never went out. At dusk, a 50 mph sustained northeast wind was blowing straight down the Hudson pushing the river over its banks. The rain fell in torrential fashion in a white wavy curtain that looked like bedsheets blowing on a clothesline. *Phyllis Lake*

Nyack, HRM 28: By 5:00 PM, the rain was coming down in sections—sheets of silver that flattened the breakers on the river with persistent 45 mph winds. In the midst of this, a kingfisher zigzagged upriver looking for a way around the wind. A great blue heron lumbered north over flattened treetops. In some places we had a foot of rain in four hours. *Daniel Wolff*

New Hamburg, HRM 67.5: By 10:00 PM, 65 mph wind gusts were coming every few minutes. We heard the sound of cannons, as large trees snapped, transformers exploded, and power lines fell. On my way to the river I had to detour—five trees had fallen across my usual route. The river was dark and, in a perfect complement, so was the shoreline as far as I could see. Power was out. The water was total blackness even though it was being tossed, thrown, and white with foam. This dark and wild scene may have been similar to the river Henry Hudson saw in September of 1609, except for a few Indian hearths. Henry never

heard a wind like this, however. The roar sounded as though a train were coming, but never arriving. *Tom Lake*

Town of Wappinger, HRM 68: *Floyd* destroyed two of our most cherished possessions: At 10:15 PM, a 60-foot, 40-inch diameter, 140-year-old sugar maple that shaded the greater part of our yard, came crashing down just missing our house; several miles away at Chelsea Yacht Club, the mooring swivel wore itself through the mooring line of our 18' Rally Bowrider in six-foot waves. It tipped to its side and the next large wave sank it. We miss them both. *Vince Francese and family*

Sharp-shinned hawk   by Wayne Kocher

Tenafly, NJ, HRM 17: More than eight inches of rain fell washing out trails at the Greenbrook Sanctuary. *Nancy Slowik*

Manhattan, HRM 0: Just after 10:00 PM, the eye of the storm moved through the New York City area, heading northeast at 30 mph. *National Weather Service*

9/17 Adirondack High Peaks, Essex County: The ancient Adirondacks have survived four ice ages, logging, even tourism. But this summer's drought and autumn's storms have taken a toll along hundreds of miles of trails that will be visible for generations. Tens of thousands of trees were blown down or uprooted by the winds and torrents of tropical storm *Floyd.* The damage was more severe partly because of dry soil and roots caused by months of severe drought. Five major landslides left by 3½" of rain in one day could forever scar the Adirondacks, where the bedrock was formed 1.2 billion years ago creating North America's

47

oldest rock formation. The NYSDEC reports that 360 miles of trails have been littered by toppled trees. The heavy rains flushed the thin layer of soil down the northwestern slope of Mount Colden; 2,500' of dirt and trees have slid to the mountain's base. The hiking trail to Marcy Dam and Lake Colden is under thirty feet of muck and branches. Perhaps appropriately, the damage is most apparent at Avalanche Pass. *Neil Zimmerman*

John Boyd Thatcher State Park, HRM 145: Thanks to tropical storm *Floyd* streams are flowing and the waterfalls are roaring. One large oak was uprooted and some tree limbs are down, but we are grateful for the rain. The waterfalls had been dry since May and there was barely a trickle in the streams all summer. Every living thing is sighing with relief. *Nancy Engel*

Town of Windham, HRM 117: Rainfall levels associated with tropical storm *Floyd* produced record levels. The *National Weather Service* reported 10.9" of rain in the Batavia Kill watershed which greatly exceeded the hundred-year-record rainfall amount of eight inches. In the upper watershed, landowners reported rainfall amounts of 10"-14". *René Van Schaack*

Westchester County: Tropical storm *Floyd* dumped ten inches of rain in 24 hours and then served up a night of gale force winds. Huge trees crashed, basements flooded, creeks turned into rivers, and schools and business stayed closed for a second day. Monarch butterflies drifted dreamily from one clump of flowers to another, colors bright and wings intact. How did they weather the storm? *Christopher Letts*

Town of Wappinger, HRM 67: In the aftermath of *Floyd,* the sky was blue, the air crisp, but 30 mph wind gusts continued as a reminder. A foot of rain had fallen from Westchester north to the Hudson Highlands across two days. My 15" rubber fishing boots that had been left out in the storm were filled to within a couple inches of the top. From the first gust of *Floyd* to the last, it would be fifty hours

before our electric and telephone were restored. *Tom Lake, Phyllis Lake*

9/18   Tenafly, NJ, HRM 17: It was another great day, sunny with a northwest wind, to observe the fall migration of birds and butterflies along the Hudson River. The Greenbrook Sanctuary took up watch from 10:00 AM to 4:00 PM. They counted 15 sharp-shinned hawks, 7 Cooper's hawks, 21 American kestrels, one merlin, 14 osprey, 7 northern harriers, 4 bald eagles (3 of them adults) and 3,618 [not a misprint] broad-winged hawks. Among the butterflies were an estimated 500 monarchs and 3 cloudless sulfur butterflies. Adding to the aerial traffic were two skeins of Canada geese, one of double-crested cormorants, and several flocks of tree swallows and chimney swifts. *Nancy Slowik, Sandy Bonardi*

9/19   Esopus Meadows, HRM 87: The river has changed color to a deep, chocolate brown from *Floyd*. The local streams have gone from dry to raging. The water chestnuts are all uprooted and lie matted on the beach. I counted 150 mute swans out on the meadows—a new record for me. Quite a few pied-billed grebes were swimming among the uprooted vegetation. *Fran Drakert, Bill Drakert*

Seining at Kowawese

9/23   Croton Point, HRM 35: Migrating monarch butterflies had been in short supply until this weekend. Tropical storm *Floyd* blew through, the first big arctic air mass of the

48

season arrived, and a flood of monarchs followed. Yesterday they were moving over the landfill at a rate of thirty an hour; today the rate increased to fifty. At midday, a joyful sight—a carpet of kestrels foraged over the landfill, sixty in sight at one time and easily the most I have observed there. *Christopher Letts*

Autumnal Equinox

9/23   Chelsea, HRM 65.2: At 6:31 AM, autumn arrived. It was 390 years ago today that Henry Hudson sailed back downriver, disappointed that his excursion up the river did not result in a passage to the Far East. *Tom Lake*

Kowawese, HRM 59: We welcomed autumn with 25 students from a *Mount Saint Mary College* program. The dazzling blue sky could not offset the mocha-brown river still silt-laden from *Floyd*. The brisk southwest breeze was making this a difficult day for migrating monarchs, but we still counted eight in an hour tacking their way down along the river, using the lee of the shoreline and the stands of tall cottonwoods to ease their headway. We spotted a pair on the rim of a puddle in the parking lot—butterflies get dehydrated just as we do on a breezy day. The river and the air were both 71°F, which made wading with our seine comfortable. It seemed the storm may have displaced some of the usual fish since our catch was meager: a few dozen *yoy* American shad, alewives, striped bass, and a delightful little three-inch largemouth bass. As we stood on the sand and talked about the many migrations occurring at this time of the year—butterflies and fish among them—I just happened to look up. There, hovering in the breeze 75' over our heads, eyeing the fish on our net, was an osprey. I think it had noticed the foot-long gizzard shad flopping in the net. But before we could make an offering it flared away in the breeze and disappeared down the beach. *Tom Lake, Leon Najman, Howard Smith, Agnes Strassner, Betty Corey*

Englewood, NJ, HRM 13.5: After more than a foot of rain the salinity had dropped from 20.0 ppt to 5.0 ppt. At Croton, 21 miles upriver, salinity went from 10.0 ppt to nonexistent, virtually overnight. *Christopher Letts*

9/24   North Germantown, HRM 109: Water temperature had dropped eight degrees overnight to 63°F. The inshore shallows were nearly devoid of fish—only one *yoy* blueback herring in the net after a dozen tries. We did catch a fair number of *yoy* American shad and alewives, but not nearly the number we caught the day before *Floyd*. In the half-hour we stretched the fifty-foot seine across the water, a dozen monarchs passed between us. The river looked every part of its big water reputation. With full moon minus one day, strong south winds were blowing directly up the river pushing the tide. A plastic bottle in midriver appeared to be almost skipping over the waves as it raced upriver in the current. Overhead, an immature bald eagle trying to make headway south had to quarter the wind and tack across the sky, no doubt expending much energy. *Bob Schmidt, Tom Lake*

Cohoes, HRM 157: The Hudson watershed was still emptying from tropical storm *Floyd*. The water was roaring over the 280' falls at Cohoes where the Mohawk River drops down to meet the Hudson at Waterford. A large deadfall was perched precariously at the lip of the falls—it had not been there a week ago. Eight daredevil cormorants had found space along the trunk and branches. Twenty feet from the crest of the falls a pair of common loons dove and swam in the face of the ferocious current, a testimony to the strength of their legs. *Tom Lake, Bob Schmidt*

Cold Spring to West Point, HRM 54-51: In the aftermath of tropical storm *Floyd* the river was awash in floating debris. As I paddled my kayak south I retrieved waterborne trash, mostly plastic bottles, styrofoam cups, candy wrappers, and spray bottles nearly filling two nylon mesh bags. In stark contrast, I saw cormorants on the river, great blue herons along the shore, and monarch butterflies in the air. *Walt Thompson*

9/25 New Hamburg, HRM 67: The full moon of September met tropical storm *Floyd,* or what remained of it. Today's high tide, enhanced by the effects of the full moon, coupled with the high and roily runoff from *Floyd,* had Wappinger Creek up in the trees. Anglers in their sleek bass boats were casting their spinnerbaits and buzzbaits into areas that were normally high and dry and, in some instances, hiking paths along the water. Throughout the day, monarchs at the rate of a hundred an hour passed by heading south. *Tom Lake*

9/26   Croton Point, HRM 34: It seemed everything with wings was in the air today. Hundreds of blue jays circled high and swung out from Sarah's Point on their way to the Palisades cliffs. Broad-winged hawks and kestrels did the same, and monarchs were passing at the rate of 35 per hour. I saw no fewer than six flocks of chickadees making their way south and west along the Point; the largest flock held more than forty birds. I saw my first fights of migratory geese, buried deep in the sky. *Christopher Letts*

Croton Point, HRM 35: *Henry Gourdine* died two years ago next month at the age of 93. Before he died, he built us a 200' seine to use in Hudson River education programs. Since Henry's passing, the net just doesn't seem to catch fish as it once did. Like a pet who has lost its owner, it just "mopes" in the water. We used to use the net and then visit Henry the next day to tell him of our catch. "Henry, we caught 200 fish in your net last night." And Henry would say, "Imagine if you guys actually knew what you were doing!" Henry was not only our mentor, but he was also our tormentor. *Tom Lake, Christopher Letts*

"Henry's seine" was built to exacting specifications: his own. He considered the one he made for us to be a "toy." He once built a 2600' commercial haul seine that used a quarter-mile of head rope. One day, fifty years ago at Crawbuckie, Henry and his crew caught 14,000 pounds of American shad and striped bass. He was not altogether happy about the haul; it took the crew so long to weigh, box, and ice the fish, that

they missed the opportunity to set on the next tide. *Christopher Letts*

Croton Point, HRM 35: We began our program at dusk, with a red sky in the west over Low Tor and a bright orange moon about to come up in the east—an idyllic setting. We set Henry's net out in the bay, made a wide semicircle, and hauled back to the beach. As the seine hit the sand, a dozen pairs of hands busily drew the seamlines in from the river. When all but the bag was on the beach, we could hear a commotion in the water: for a change the bag was seething with life. In one short haul we had caught over 600 fish, nearly 400 of which were small Atlantic menhaden. A juvenile weakfish was tenderly lifted for all to see in the lantern light and then released. In the post-*Floyd* river, salinity was way down (2.0 ppt on this night) and so we were not surprised when we found a white sucker, a freshwater fish in the net. There was a mix of 150 *yoy* striped bass and white perch, as well as fifty juvenile bluefish. The blues were likely pursuing the bass and perch. We also caught 14 blue crabs, several of which came in with double-fisted snacks: a *yoy* bass or perch in each claw. The water was a cool 68°F. *Craig Paupst, April Paupst, Ann Marie Dolan, Charles Herman, Kristy Herman*

P.S. We tagged and released a 22", four-pound striped bass from the beach on this night. The bass was recaptured on May 15, 2000 by *James Wight* at Normandy Beach, New Jersey. This location is 32 miles south of Sandy Hook, one-half mile south of Manasquan Inlet. It was free for 232 days and traveled 85 miles.

9/28   Foundry Cove, HRM 53: With my eyes focused on the hordes of mallards and a few great blue herons in the marsh, I was almost startled as I turned around to look up the hillside. The sky was filled with huge black birds. There were dozens of turkey vultures banking and soaring on upturned wings. I scanned the kettles with my binoculars hoping to single out a black vulture or a red-tailed hawk, but every one was a turkey vulture. Because there were so many of them, I felt obligated to count them. There were 61. *Rich Anderson*

9/29   Dobbs Ferry, HRM 23: Our beach seine was filled with nearly 600 fish—snapper blues, white perch, a vast school of silverside, and several 4"-7" striped bass. For whatever reason this year's crop of striped bass is running 2-3 times the average size for this time of the year. Low flying monarchs passed in twos and threes, dipping within inches, brushing against us, as they beat into strong southerlies. The students from Irvington were thrilled to be so close to so much loveliness. As they passed, the students called out the tally; they were moving past us at the rate of fifty per hour. *Christopher Letts*

Bear Mountain, HRM 46: The Bear Mountain Bridge is a crossing point for many flocks of small birds migrating south in autumn. And the peregrine falcon is the "toll taker." Peregrine falcons have flourished on this bridge throughout the 1990s, reproducing and having a year around presence. Between migrations of songbirds, there is always a supply of pigeons and other prey. *Wayne Kocher, Christopher Letts*

Mid-Hudson Valley: September 1999 was the fourth warmest and fifth wettest September in the last 104 years. The summer drought had abated. *John Thompson, Mohonk Lake Cooperative Research Station*

Turkey vulture   by Wayne Kocher

October 1999

Nothing ever really goes to waste in an estuary.
When a plant or animal dies, bacteria, shrimps, crabs, eels,
and other scavengers feed upon it and help recycle the nutrients.
The rocking action of the tides keeps the lower Hudson stirred
like a thick soup.
Robert H. Boyle, The Hudson, A Natural and Unnatural History

10/1   Rosetown, HRM 65.4: *Lawson Upchurch*, of Normandeau Associates, found two more fat sleepers (36-40 mm) from the Rosetown impingement collection. Others had been caught previously on September 10 and 24. *Bob Daniels*

Fat sleeper is a salt water fish that, on occasion, strays into the Hudson. *C. Lavett Smith* describes the fat sleeper as a "stubby little fish" (Smith 1985:442) that are closely related to the gobies. We have three species of goby in the Hudson, of which only the naked goby is anywhere near common. Fat sleepers, like many tropical marine strays, are much more common in the Caribbean.

Yonkers to Peekskill, HRM 18-44: The 150th anniversary of the Hudson River Railroad Line from New York City to Peekskill was celebrated with special train rides between Yonkers and Peekskill. Metro North Railroad took two diesels out of mothballs, repainted them with the distinctive New York Central colors and logos and provided two observation cars and new cars for the historic trip. Hundreds of passengers were delighted by the large clean windows and the opportunity to see the Hudson River so clearly. *Lyn Roessler*

Piermont, HRM 25: Out on the very tip of Piermont Pier, anglers were tossing cast nets for bait. Large bluefish and schoolie-sized striped bass were around and a live menhaden was a hot bait. One net landed over a school of 4"-5" silvery fish with yellow tails. They were not "bunker." The fishermen had no idea what they were, so they showed me one. These were crevalle jacks (115 mm), a tropical fish. *Bob Gabrielson.*

Poughkeepsie, HRM 74: I am still consistently getting 33-35 dozen blue crabs, every other day, in my seventy pots. Halfway through the lift today, I spotted a small kettle of five red-tailed hawks over Blue Point. Among them was a raven. The hawks managed to gingerly soar in their kettle, avoiding the big black bird. Water temperature was 68°F. *John Mylod*

10/4   Essex County, HRM 315: The first snow of the season, up to four inches, fell overnight, in the High Peaks. *National Weather Service*

Croton Point, HRM 34.5: Observations from the Point included a Baird's sandpiper, upland sandpipers mixed in with killdeer, and a pectoral sandpiper. *Larry Bickford* has been seeing monarchs passing through at an estimated rate of 500 per hour. *Christopher Letts*

Coyote   by Wayne Kocher

10/6   Tenafly, NJ, HRM 17: A skein of snow geese, fifty birds, passed over today heading downriver. Two peregrine falcons coursed the Palisades. *Nancy Slowik*

10/7   Cornwall, HRM 56: The NYSDEC Hudson River Fisheries Unit was seining the river at Cornwall. Among their catch was a highfin goby (77 mm). This was a new species for the Hudson, number 209. *Scott Davis, Amanda Cosman, John O'Connor*

This **highfin goby**, our first, is a tropical marine stray in the Hudson. It was a surprising catch even in the midst of a hundred-year drought that has increased Hudson River salinity. The highfin goby, formerly known as the sharptail goby, is found from the Caribbean to North Carolina. This one was significantly north of its range. It was identified by *Bob Schmidt* (Walls 1975: 326).

Croton Point, HRM 35: The west end of the bathing beach collects everything that comes down the east shore of the river. At low tide I like to wade out and inspect the treasures collected by the currents of wind and water that wash the Point. Today I picked up yet another pair of swim goggles, slimy and discolored. Inside one of the eyepieces was a thumbnail-sized jingle shell, testimony to the intrusion of the marine environment this year. *Christopher Letts*

Jingle shells are a bivalve mollusk, like a clam or an oyster. Unlike these, however, their two valves (shells) are dissimilar in shape. The upper valve is a thin, glossy, translucent shell. The lower valve is flat with a large hole. There are very few reports of jingle shells from the lower Hudson. These could be another drought-induced presence. The empty valves are a common component of "sea shell" collections along the Atlantic Coast from Cape Cod to the Carolinas.

Croton River, HRM 34: I collected an exceptionally large wedge rangia (55 mm), a brackish-water clam, in the Croton River today. *Christopher Letts*

Wedge rangia is a bivalve mollusk native to more southerly, brackish, coastal and inshore waters such as Delaware Bay and Chesapeake Bay. It is believed that they were inadvertently introduced to the Hudson River about 15 years ago through the ballast water of commercial vessels. This particular clam exceeded the cited maximum size for the species (Gosner 1971:315).

Beach seining   by Phyllis Lake

Englewood, NJ, HRM 13.5: The loose rocks buttressing the northernmost fishing jetty at the Englewood Boat Basin have always been a good collecting place for shrimp and small crabs. I can say with some surety that the Japanese green crabs were not there in the autumn of 1998 or in the spring of 1999 when I turned boulders there. Today each sizeable rock harbored 2-6 of the crabs, males and females, 18-20 mm carapace width. A bit later, moulted shells of the crabs came up in the beach seine. The crabs are fast and agile. One specimen slipped through a crack in the top of the picnic table and I scrambled underneath looking for it on the ground. When I could not find it, I looked up at the bottom of the tabletop and there was the crab clinging to the flat surface of the wood. They have a spider-like appearance and at first glance remind me of a tarantula. *Christopher Letts, Alon Gordon*

Japanese green crabs were first identified in the Hudson River by *Miguel Padilla* in the summer of 1994. Those crabs were captured at Pier 26 on the lower west side of Manhattan at river mile 1.

10/8   Kowawese, HRM 59: We had an overnight temperature in the high 20s producing heavy frost on the windshield this morning. When the sun peaked over Breakneck Ridge it provided instant warming. There were long, heavy tiderows of wild celery on the beach, normal for autumn's die-off, but thicker due to the tidal surge effect of tropical storm *Floyd*. This provided a banquet table several spotted sandpipers. The lower edge of the beach, the last ten feet to the water's edge, was primarily gravel. The runoff and ebbing tide from *Floyd* had sorted out and taken much of the sand. *Tom Lake*

Englewood, NJ, HRM 13.5: I don't think of wrens as birds that flock, but there was a crowd of winter wrens foraging in the warm sunlight at the Englewood Boat Basin today. At least twenty of the birds were in and out of cracks in the rock walls, under the picnic tables, and along the lawn boarding the parking lot. *Christopher Letts*

10/9   Athens, HRM 115: From Cohotate Preserve on the Hudson we watched a pair of immature bald eagles soaring overhead. Waterfowlers seemed to be everywhere. Strings of decoys were set along the shore in the shallows, blinds were scattered about, and occasionally *"pop-pop-pop"* would fill the air. Several small flocks of blue-winged teal and black ducks circled and landed. Several monarchs caught a tail wind and fluttered past. We were told by some local residents that the "crick eels" were on the move. This left us quite puzzled. The water temperature was 59°F. *Noah Wadden, Andy Turner, Jon Powell, Christopher Letts, Tom Lake*

Crick eels are apparently "bigger and tastier than river eels." One gentleman, to emphasize this point, held his hand 3½' off the ground, which equaled their length. He cupped his hands together to make a five-inch diameter circle to show big around they are. We concluded that these were mature American eels descending tributaries from ponds, lakes, reservoirs in the fall. *Henry Gourdine* used to call these big female spawners "silver eels." Many eels leave the estuary in late autumn to spawn at sea.

Croton Point, HRM 34-35: The *Saw Mill River Audubon Society* made some interesting sightings during a hike of the point: an immature clay-colored sparrow, Lincoln's sparrow, white-crowned sparrow, Cape May warbler, myrtle warblers, palm warblers, two blackpoll warblers, sharp-shinned hawk, Cooper's hawk, kestrels, and some American water pipits.

10/11 Kowawese, HRM 59: A monarch fluttered down the beach as we prepared to haul our eighty-foot seine. It reminded us of the season when birds, fish, and butterflies are on the move to wintering locations. We hauled just once and caught several hundred small fish, the overwhelming majority of which were *yoy* migrating downriver. We interrupted them only long enough to show a few around in a small glass jar, and then eased the net back into the river to allow them all to continue on their way. Many of them were herring—five species. Most were bluebacks, but there were also American shad, alewives, and two nonmigratory herring, Atlantic menhaden and gizzard shad. The latter, although only four inches long, reminded us that adult gizzard shad are prime forage for wintering bald eagles. There were three dozen three-inch striped bass, a good indication of yet another successful year class for the species. *Marc Moran, Fran Dunwell, Steve Stanne, Betsy Blair, Harold King, Tom Lake*

10/12 North Germantown, HRM 109: The river was a chilly 57°F, about 7° colder than on this date last October. A couple monarchs fluttered past, one flutter ahead of the next serious frost. We continued to be puzzled by the number of small yoy (55 mm) striped bass—truly a late hatch.. Each haul also netted scores of tiny blue crabs the size of nickels and dimes. We thought it was pretty far upriver for these guys (they were overwhelmingly male).

We found a seven-inch striped bass lying dead along the tideline. A small tail was protruding from its jaws. The bass had tried to swallow a quarter-sized redbreast sunfish, got it halfway down, changed its mind, and then could not spit it out. Sunfish have a spiny second dorsal fin that erects when pushed backward. Dead striped bass on the beach, having choked on sunfish or perch, are not a rare sight. As we were gathering our net to move twenty miles upriver to Mill Creek we heard a soft chorus of *"Cr-r-r-r-uk, cr-r-r-r-uk."* We stood and watched as a lazy V of more than 200 brant passed low over our heads. *Bob Schmidt, Tom Lake*

Mill Creek, HRM 129: It was low tide at the mouth of Mill Creek where not much more than a trickle meandered across several hundred feet of mud flats to the receded river. The rocks exposed by the tide were completely covered with zebra mussels—a plankton trap. How much was getting out of this tributary? We watched a greater yellowlegs feed in the remnant creek as it ran through thin stands of three-square sedge. It was catching small silvery fish in the swift water and then dashing over to the sandy bank to drop, turn, and swallow them. Once it appeared to catch and consume a small blue crab. *Bob Schmidt, Tom Lake*

Kayaker at Storm King Mountain by Walt Thompson

Cohoes, HRM 157: The long reach of the Mohawk near the crest of the Cohoes Falls was quiet one moment, then raucous the next. Hundreds of gulls were lifting off the water and dispersing in all directions. Overhead, a kettle of two dozen turkey vultures parted—every vulture for themselves. We knew what it was even before we saw the perpetrator: an adult bald eagle slowly flapping its way across the top of

the falls and disappearing into the treeline. Within a minute order was resumed, the gulls came back, and the kettle reformed overhead. A half-dozen monarchs passed over in their own miniature version of a kettle. *Tom Lake, Bob Schmidt*

Blue Point, HRM 74: The pots held twelve dozen keeper blue crabs (at least 5½" carapace width) with an additional 15-20 dozen smaller throwbacks. Out of 350-380 crabs, only 5 were females. Eight red-tailed hawks soared and played in the thermals rising off the rocky face of Blue Point. In a repeat of nine days ago, a lone raven flew among them. *John Mylod*

Sandy Hook, NJ: The brant were back. Every year we can almost count on brant leaving Sandy Hook on Memorial Day for northern nesting territory, and then returning on Columbus Day as they fly south to wintering grounds. *Dery Bennett*

Kowawese, HRM 59: The stiff westerly breeze at dawn had intensified into a 35 mph northwest wind. A couple of monarchs came down the beach and they were not "fluttering." They were being whisked along, almost effortlessly. It was low tide at 9:30 AM. At 12:30 PM, the tide was still dropping, being blown out by the wind. We were having a blowout tide. Students from *Sheafe Road Elementary* helped seine the shallows along the beach after which we examined our catch in the lee of a small terrace. Many were baby fish on their way to downriver: American shad, blueback herring, alewives, and striped bass. While releasing *yoy* blueback herring a belted kingfisher swooped down, picked one off the water, and continued on its way. Several of the large rocks, now exposed by the falling tide, were covered with barnacles, a testimony to the spring and summer drought. Barnacles, a brackish water crustacean, require a low level of salt in the water. In fall of 1997, after a dry summer, a large deadfall washed up on this beach. It was covered end-to-end with large barnacles (see Kowawese, IV:43). The water temperature was 58°F. *Gene Martin, Sue Bride,*

Bev Bischoff, Lisa Taliber, Nicole Donovan, Phyllis Lake, Tom Lake

Blowout tides are not common. They occur most frequently following several days of strong and steady north-northwest winds. The daily tidal flushing of the estuary begins to accumulate a "net loss" of high water as the progression of flood tides are unable to compensate for ebb tides that are being lengthened in duration and effect by the wind. If this happens around a new or full moon (spring tides) the result can be even more spectacular. This scenario culminates in an ebb tide that seems to go seaward forever, draining tidemarshes and inshore shallows until prehistoric flood plains and a glimpse of "the bottom of the river" is exposed.

10/15 Hudson River, Lock 1, HRM 164.5: The river was full of *yoy* blueback herring. This time last year it seemed all of them had left for the ocean by now. *Everett Nack, Smokey Schools*

10/16 Manhattan, HRM 1: A juvenile gray snapper was captured at The River Project's Pier 26. This is a rare catch in the Hudson; probably fewer than a dozen have been reported over the years. The salinity was 23.0 ppt; water temperature was 59°F. *Cathy Drew*

10/17 Town of Esopus, HRM 87: While we would still hear a chorus of coyotes and screech owls, this would be the last day this fall that we would note hearing katydids in our daily log. *Fran Drakert and Bill Drakert*

Croton Point, HRM 34.5: I counted 13 eastern meadowlarks on the landfill. In a flock, they were easily flushed but the grasses are too high to see them when they land. A migrating goshawk also flushed from a tree and headed southwest out across the river. *Larry Bickford*

10/20 Poughkeepsie, HRM 74: As I was checking my crab pots, a mat of water milfoil and wild celery floated past in the current. An adult blue crab swam up, grabbed on, and was carried downriver in the ebb tide. It seemed to me that it was a conscious effort to hitch a ride. My pots held eight dozen keeper crabs (one was

7½"). I tossed back 15-20 dozen shorts. There was a huge white perch (12") in one pot, along with three species of catfish: channel cat, white cat, and brown bullhead. There was a big crayfish in one pot, tearing at the bait well. Hundreds of tiny, penny-sized, bug crabs *(yoy)* were also picking at the bait in most of the pots. Along the shore I could hear a Carolina wren and a mockingbird. The water was 60°F, and it was a beautiful day. *John Mylod*

Croton Point, HRM 35: We watched several spotted sandpipers, both in the air and walking along the sea wall. They were in winter plumage nervously working their way across the breakwater, as though "teetering"—a good field mark (see Peterson 1980:132). We pulled the seine through the shallows that were now void of wild celery and water milfoil—fish habitat. The storm surge from tropical storm *Floyd* had finished uprooting it all. As we slid the net up on the beach and opened the bag for all to see—sixty pairs of sixth grade eyes—it was empty! What an embarrassingly humble haul. We did our best to explain the vagaries of the river and the value of an "empty net," how it is often more important to contemplate what you did *not* catch. We then sent the net back through the shallows, this time with a bit more determination. Minutes later we were rewarded with a bag full of *yoy* blueback herring, alewives, and American shad, all on their way to sea. The water was 58°F and the salinity was 2.2 ppt. *Tom Lake, Christopher Letts, Liz DeAngelis*

Beach seining offers a wonderful opportunity to introduce people to the fauna of the Hudson and to teach about the estuarine ecosystem. We pride ourselves on careful handling of the catch and preach the gospel of the sanctity of life as we sort specimens while kneeling right in the swash. The problem is, every student's gut instinct is to dive in and grab a fish. Human nature, pure and simple. Hard lessons have taught us that this cannot be allowed. The ensuing free-for-all is just as deadly to the educational intent as it is to river creatures. Luckily there exists the eel. Stories abound of the toughness of this common fish, how they can travel overland, and have been known to survive a night on a dry and dusty classroom floor after effecting an escape from an aquarium. I have no qualms about lining the kids up and letting them try to pick up an adult eel out of a five-gallon bucket (only one hand, please!). After that, the eel race. A true win/win scenario. The kids get to touch a fish, the eel swims free, and I don't feel guilty about having had all of the fun. *Christopher Letts*

Beach seining eel races   by Phyllis Lake

Sandy Hook, NJ: This morning Sandy Hook was alive with thousands of kinglets, ruby-crowned and golden-crowned, as well as white-throated and white-crowned sparrows, yellow-rumped warblers, and phoebes. This is what birders call a "fall out," when songbirds that have flying all night drop down on land and feed. *Dery Bennett*

10/23 Bay Ridge Flats, New York Harbor: In the afternoon we sailed out of Liberty State Park into the Upper Bay to use our fishing trawl. After spending most of the month up the river it was a treat to see some saltier species. We caught a tautog, 4 scup, 15 blue crabs, 4 lady crabs, and a lined sea horse. An odd looking slender fish stood out amongst the others in our onboard aquarium. After some deliberation and with much excitement, we pronounced it to be an inshore lizardfish. I had never even heard of a lizardfish! What a reminder of the vast secrets that the estuary veils in her waters; how fortunate we are to be graced with even the slightest glimpse. *Sean Madden*

Lady Crabs, like the blue crab, have a flattened pair of legs that they use to scuddle about. These "paddles" make them swimming crabs. Unlike the blue crab, which is a resident species in the Hudson from the lower estuary to Troy, the lady crab is more of a marine animal. As much as a blue crab will try to rip off your finger nails if you are not careful, it is possible that the lady crab is even more ill-tempered. My golden retriever once stuck her inquisitive snout into a foamy swell at Sandy Hook and came up yelping with a lady crab stuck on her nose. When wading in shallows, blue crabs will swim away if you come near. Lady crabs will pinch your toes. *Tom Lake*

10/27 Middle Ground Flats, HRM 119.5: Canada geese and an assortment of ducks were rafting in the lee of the Middle Ground. The river was capping over in the face of a strong west wind; every few hundred yards a raft of Canadas, numbering at least one hundred birds, were huddled in the chop out of the waves. Three or four flocks circled overhead looking to set down, not sure if there was room, hoping to rotate with those already on the water. Skeins of cormorants were coming south paralleling the railroad tracks. *Gail Mihocko, Stephanie Matteson, Tom Lake*

Hudson North Bay, HRM 119: This was an ebb tide being driven by a strong west wind and a near-full moon. The high marsh was draining through scores of tiny rivulets; the low marsh was emptying via tidal creeks. Pond lily stalks and pondweed leaves streamed out under the trestle to the river. A female kingfisher hopped from telephone pole to telephone pole staying ahead of me as I walked along the railroad tracks. Her raucous squawk let me know that I was invading her space. A small congregation of black ducks drifted in one of the creeks finding the low water level an advantage to feeding. Fifty rock doves flew past in synchronized flight. Red-winged blackbirds wheeled overhead and mockingbirds perched in pairs along the marsh. But unlike such an assemblage in spring, the air was still, the scene was quiet—silence, the birdsong of autumn. Except for the kingfisher! Back down the marsh she came, stopping dead still in the air. She hovered on beating wings like a hummingbird, for five, ten seconds, dropped like a pelican to the water, then rose with a killifish. Moments later the tone of the marsh changed: gulls scattered, crows cawed and flew low out over the river, the red-wings dove into the phragmites, and the pigeons left quickly as well. Overhead an immature bald eagle made its way over the marsh and, with a tail wind, disappeared to the east. *Tom Lake*

Tom Lake with winter flounder   by Phyllis Lake

Poughkeepsie, HRM 75: The day began sunny and calm but by afternoon, as the tide turned to flood, the sky grew gray and the northwest wind began to blow straight down the river. Amidst four-foot waves, I "crabbed" my way across the river, tending to my pots. There were ten dozen keeper blue crabs and a like number of throwbacks—too small. A dozen

white catfish had found refuge in my pots; some of them were huge. In some pots there were more fish than crabs: white suckers, white perch, brown bullheads. The river was 55°F. *John Mylod*

10/28 Englewood, NJ, HRM 13.5: On a perfect flying day the sky was filled with vultures. In half an hour, 45 of them spiraled high above the Palisades cliffs and bore off to the south, mirroring the scores of migrating shad and other herring we had just seined out of the Hudson. The birds have a wingspan of up to seven feet, I told my school kids, and what we were seeing is called a "kettle" of vultures. One suggested that, since it was almost Halloween, we should call it a "cauldron" of vultures! *Christopher Letts*

10/29 Englewood, NJ, HRM 13.5: While we waited for students from *New York University* to arrive for a Hudson River education program, we sat and watched a female ruby-crowned kinglet flit from shrub to shrub looking for berries. Two pipevine swallowtail butterflies floated past and several broad-winged hawks swung out lazily just below the rim of the Palisades, finessing a thermal. The students helped us seine and they were fascinated when the bag came ashore. It was filled with *yoy* American shad, striped bass, bay anchovies, Atlantic silverside, gizzard shad, sand shrimp, shore shrimp, and fifty blue crabs the size of nickels and quarters. We found many ribbed mussels on exposed rocks below the reach of the tide. Under most of the rocks were Japanese green crabs. Everything seemed pretty normal for river mile 13.5 in late October—salinity 11.7 ppt, water temperature 55°F—except for a dozen cowrie shells we found on the beach at the tideline. Cowries are a southerly, deepwater mollusk. We were at a loss to explain how they got there. *Brendon Walsh, Gretchen Bowman, Rie Akazawa, Brian Derr, Adam Weiner, Christopher Letts, Tom Lake*

Aliens: We were displaying recent and inadvertent additions to the fauna of the estuary to some *New York University* students: zebra mussels, wedge clams, and the very new Japanese green crabs. As the discussion wound down, a Japanese-American student charmed us with this story: "Would you like to know how we eat them in Japan? First we put them in a bowl of sake until they are tipsy. Then we cook them in a very hot oil. Finally, we eat all of them; they are small and crispy." Instantly, a whole new perspective was created. *Christopher Letts*

10/30 Englewood, NJ, HRM 13.5: As it had the day before, arriving early always has its rewards. Today we sat and watched Cape May warblers, magnolia warblers, and black-throated green warblers, working through the shrubbery along the shore. Several pipevine swallowtail butterflies came by, landed on the blooming Japanese honeysuckle, and then drifted away down the beach. Overhead an osprey banked in circles using a thermal and a westerly breeze to edge out over the river. Reminding us that our seasons were meeting, summer-to-autumn-to-winter, we spotted a pair of snow buntings in eclipse plumage hoping along the sandy beach. *Roger Tory Peterson* called these birds, along with the juncos, "snowbirds." We seined the shallows with the Greenbrook Sanctuary, thigh-deep in a compost heap. The bottom was an accumulation of decades of decaying leaves and other organics. Seasons were meeting in the river as well: 7 winter flounder were mixed in with 75 *yoy* American shad and striped bass, heading to sea. A few sand shrimp were popping and at least thirty "bugs" were scurrying all over the damp net—baby blue crabs the size of

pennies. We also found some empty oyster valves (35 mm) on the beach, evidence of live oysters just out beyond the reach of low tide. Salinity was 12.1 ppt; water temperature was 55°F. *Sandy Bonardi, Phyllis Lake, Tom Lake, Christopher Letts*

10/31 High Peaks Region, Essex County: The weather was fair with increasing clouds in the late afternoon. The ground was beginning to freeze with ice on the trails to Gray and Skylight peaks. Nighttime temperatures were below freezing. The daytime high was only 38°F. In the aftermath of the dry summer weather and the heavy rains and winds of tropical storm *Floyd,* there was significant blowdown from Uphill Brook, along the Opalescent, quite extensive along Feldspar Brook about two miles below Lake Tear. The water spilling from Lake Tear was clear and free of any visible debris. *Cheryl Esper, John Esper*

Englewood, NJ, HRM 13.5: There was another meeting of the seasons on the beach today. Our seine came ashore with two dozen *yoy* striped bass, American shad, and blue crabs, typical of our autumn migration. In among all these smaller fish was a larger one, the length of my palm, a beautiful crevalle jack. This was a fish of the warmer and saltier waters of summer. Salinity was 12.2 ppt; water temperature was 54°F. *Christopher Letts, Jennifer March*

November 1999

The large oysters are proper for roasting and stewing.
Each of these will fill a spoon, and make a good bite.
I have seen many in the shell a foot long and broad in proportion.
Adrien Van der Donck, *on Hudson River Oysters, 1656*

11/1 Englewood, NJ, HRM 13.5: Three dozen third graders from the *Willard School* in Ridgefield, NJ, looked skyward with us to watch a kettle of red-tailed hawks rise and turn in the warm thermals of the Palisades. Our seine caught a few *yoy* blueback herring, American shad, and striped bass, heading seaward, still one step ahead of winter. Later, in an extreme low tide, we went "mud-larking," searching and probing the tide flats and looking under rocks. As we did, a half-dozen Japanese green crabs scurried away. We found at least a hundred small oysters (15-30 mm) on the underside of small rocks. Along 150' of exposed beach we found more cowrie shells, balthic macoma valves, soft-shelled clams, ribbed mussels (to 48 mm), and bladder wrack draped on all the rocks below mean high tide. *Denise Beirne, Tom Moran, Jayson Porrod, Tom Lake, Christopher Letts*

Barred owl   by Esther Kiviat

11/4 Queens, New York City: Bravely sailing over Gino's Pizzeria in Howard Beach, a Cooper's hawk made difficult headway against a brisk wind and what seemed to be a hundred angry crows and starlings. The bird flew southbound past 159th Avenue, over the local pizzeria and disappeared behind the Shell service station dragging crows and starlings like a comet's tail. *Dave Taft*

11/6 Croton Point, HRM 34.5: Everything was flying on this balmy, blue-sky day. More winter ducks had arrived overnight and warblers and other small songbirds were mighty scarce. A flock of greater yellowlegs poked and teetered around in a rain puddle. The same branch on the same cottonwood that has been a favorite eagle perch the last three winters was occupied again. Overhead, an air traffic controller would have been useful. Flock after flock of birds zoomed over. Most of the flocks were mixed: grackles joined red-winged blackbirds; big flocks of cowbirds mixed with cedar waxwings. The Ralph Waterman Bird Club shared a merlin sighting with me and told of seeing a mixed flock of robins and evening grosbeaks. An hour later I was admiring the precision flying of a large flock of cedar waxwings, and trying to get a count, when the tightly packed flock shattered and dove for the deck. A merlin appeared, dove, came up empty, and headed out across the Tappan Zee. Most of the time ospreys, turkey vultures, and red-tailed hawks were in view. *Christopher Letts*

11/11 Croton Point, HRM 34: I had been seeing horned grebes for two weeks, always well offshore and secretive. There is at least one that is not so secretive. Today I was shown several excellent close-up photographs by *Oren*

Smith of a horned grebe. As I admired the photos, I was told that the bird was within twenty feet of the camera and that angler *Midgie Taube* had enticed the bird even closer by feeding it live killifish. Where had it learned to associate humans and food? The bird is locally famous now and has returned at least twice daily to be fed by other fishermen. *Christopher Letts*

Marsh hawk   by Wayne Kocher

Philipse Manor, HRM 30: Our NYSDEC striped bass survey crew caught a lookdown in our seine today. This delicate little fish (76 mm) was so thin I found it hard to believe that it could survive at all. Normally a marine fish, this member of the jack family was captured in water with a salinity of only 3.5 ppt. *Ron Gelardi, Kim McKown, Matt Graff, Susan Olsen*

Lookdowns are a member of a colorful, tropical-looking, family of fishes, the jacks. Other jacks found in the Hudson estuary are permit, crevalle jack, and Atlantic moonfish. All are seasonally present, in varying numbers, from late summer though fall. Their presence is, in part, attributable to the Gulf Stream's northerly flow that carries eggs and larvae from southern waters. Lookdowns get their name from their profile; they appear to be looking down their snout as they swim about.

11/12 Troy, HRM 153.4: Using a push-net at the federal lock at Troy, we bait-netted three

pails of golden shiners. The river was boiling with *yoy* blueback herring on their way down from the Mohawk River on their way to the sea. *Everett Nack, Smokey Schools*

"Pails of bait" is a colloquial measure for minnows in the bait trade. While it is somewhat inexact, it generally translates to about a gallon of baitfish (minnies, shiners, and blue-banded mudminnows) in a five-gallon bucket.

Jamaica Bay, Queens, NY: It was an incredibly warm day for mid-November. Two bats were hunting the parking lot of the Jamaica Bay National Wildlife Refuge. One looked to be a red bat; the other was a little brown myotis. We tossed stones in the air to lure them closer. *Dave Taft*

11/15 Athens, HRM 115: It was a cool but sunny day. I spotted an adult bald eagle at the extreme northeast end of the Columbia-Greene County Community College Field Station's dock. It perched there, facing the river, as though it owned the world, until the crows noticed! *Jon Powell*

George's Island, HRM 39: A dead red fox lay in the path near the lower parking lot. The animal was well-furred and well-fleshed, and had been recently killed. We tend to think of foxes as predator, not prey, but this one had been someone's dinner—part of the hindquarters and viscera had been eaten. I've had daytime looks at coyotes at this spot twice, and parks' workers tell me that they hear howling every time a siren goes off. *Christopher Letts*

The first **coyote sighting** at the park was on a bald eagle survey day (see George's Island (Vol.II:96). It was cold, colder than zero, and I never got out of my car. I watched the moon drop and light up the eagles perched on Dogan Point. Then the sun came up, my coffee was gone. I put my car in reverse, looked in the rear view mirror, and watched a black coyote trot across the parking lot forty feet behind me and disappear in the underbrush at Swan Pond. *Christopher Letts*

11/17   Croton Bay, HRM 35: From the low tide shore we counted 140 ruddy ducks bunched together in the calm water. We could see a mixed raft of lesser scaup and ruddys silhouetted to the west near Sarah's Point. Five common mergansers were diving and surfacing near the Croton train trestle at the mouth of the Croton River, and four canvasbacks swam nearby. Away from the water we followed two snow buntings up the gravel path of the landfill. Their mostly white plumage with pale brown markings and flecks of black would give them good camouflage in a weedy field covered with snow. *Amy Silberkleit, Michael Shiffer, Isis Shiffer, Elijah Shiffer*

11/18 Croton Point, HRM 34.5: Flying right down the channel like scudding snow, a flock of snow geese was wasting no time. The first I'd seen this season. To think of where they've come from, and where they are going, just gives me the tingles. I feel honored to share the same space with migrant travelers above and beneath the waters of the Hudson. *Christopher Letts*

11/19 Upper Nyack, HRM 29: The air was 60°F and the river was 48°. I saw my first winter ducks of the season, a half-dozen buffleheads. At low tide I watched a huge snapping turtle walk across the bottom of a riverside boat yard leaving claw and tail marks in the mud. *Daniel Wolff*

On the beach, In the water
Happy as a moose
Under a blue sky,
Doggies enjoy the cool water,
The soft rolling water.
On the beach people left things that were
Not meant to kill fish, but they did.
Brendan Delaney, Pearl River Middle School, NY

Hastings-on-Hudson, HRM 21.5: The Palisades, looming skyward across the Hudson here, had a long tradition as a nesting site for peregrine falcons. The tradition was interrupted after 1951, the last year when two chicks hatched on a cliff visible from my vantage point. Decimated by DDT, the peregrine disappeared as a breeding species in the U.S. east of the Mississippi. Thanks in part to a ban on the pesticide, this princely falcon returned to the river 37 years later, nesting on the Tappan Zee Bridge in 1988, and at many more sites since. I was reminded of this today when a beautiful adult peregrine flew directly overhead following the Westchester shoreline south. *Steve Stanne*

11/21 Hi Tor, HRM 35: On the trail to the summit of High Tor. *Aldo Leopold* once wrote: "...and at long last only the hills will know," of the fading memory of the extinct passenger pigeon. Here, now, we were bearing witness to another dying species, the eastern hemlock, dying regularly, at the hands of the woolly adelgid, an insect. That was the low point of my hike. The high point was, well, the high point, High Tor. At 830', it is the highest point on the Palisades, and with commanding views of the Hudson River. In the lee of a rock I found a cadmium-yellow wildflower—alpine goldenrod. Death, life, and death again on the descending trail. It was a cedar waxwing, its neck bearing the execution mark of a raptor, which apparently had no further use for it. *Jim Capossela*

Hemlock woolly adelgid is an insect of Asian origin that has killed many stands of eastern hemlock along the tidal Hudson and its tributaries since it was first found in Westchester County in 1987. Latitude and elevation seem to be limiting factors to its distribution in the Hudson Valley.

Croton Bay, HRM 34: There was no wind but the water was anything but calm. As far as I could see, lunate ripples revealed the presence of vast schools of small menhaden, "penny bunker," in the riverman's jargon. The rippled surface was punctuated by huge boils and explosive splashes made by feeding striped bass as they chased the menhaden into the shallows. I waded to the limits of my chest waders and my second cast was blasted by a ten-pound bass. And here came at least six more schools—at last, in the right place at the right time! As I cast to the approaching fish, a major backlash developed in my reel. All I could do was watch in awe as torrents of baitfish poured past, and the feeding surrounded me. It was a moment for memory. *Christopher Letts*

11/23 Wappinger Creek, HRM 67.5: It was unseasonably warm at dawn, in the 50°s, later to be 75°F. Autumn continued to slip away as the sights and sounds of winter filtered in. Eight hen common mergansers, with their shock of red head feathers and trim silhouettes, dove in the shallows of the creek—sometimes all eight at once—for fish and crayfish. In a creekside shrub I could hear *"Old Sam Peabody, Peabody, Peabody."* The white-throated sparrows had come back for the winter. *Tom Lake*

Croton Bay, HRM 34: I was drifting my bunker net trying to get some large menhaden but what I came up with was a loon! I got it in the boat and threw my jacket over it, and then cut the bird out of the net with my knife. It looked at me for a couple minutes and then dove overboard and disappeared. *Midgie Taube*

Sandy Hook, NJ: I watched a crow pick up a clam off the tide flats, fly up to the road, and then drop it onto the blacktop to break it open. Had this crow learned this behavior, or was it mimicking the local herring gulls? *Pat Coren*

ALS Tag #500,0000   by Dery Bennett

11/26 New York Harbor, Upper Bay: The day was unusually warm at 64°F. Fog shrouded New York Harbor, the Verrazano Narrows was obscured, and light rain fell as we entered the Upper Bay from the East River aboard the charter boat *Passtime Princess*. This was the

eighth annual *Friends of Fishes* striped bass tag release outing. For the next five hours we made numerous drifts across Bay Ridge Flats, Robbins Reef, past Ellis Island, Liberty Island, and Governor's Island. Our tally was 66 bass, 63 of which we tagged and released. A single eleven-inch windowpane flounder was also taken. The highlight of the day was applying American Littoral Society tag number 500,000. At 12:04 PM, as we drifted across Robbins Reef, a 23⅛" striped bass took *Carl Marchese's* bait. Within minutes, Carl landed the fish, it was carefully tagged with number 500,000, measured, photographed, and returned to the harbor. A while later, at the north end of Bay Ridge Flats, *Pam Carlsen* caught a 22" bass, that was also tagged and released. The water temperature was 53°F. *Rogib Yazgi, Dery Bennett, John Waldman, Dave Taft, Dennis Suszkowski, Phyllis Lake, Tom Lake*

In eight years, 208 anglers in the **Friends of Fishes** program have captured, tagged, and released 394 striped bass. Twenty-three have subsequently been recaptured from as far north as Wareham, Ipswich, and New Bedford, Massachusetts, and from as far south as Barnegat, NJ. Some have been free as many as 1,066 days, and some as few as 110 days.

11/28 Yonkers, HRM 18: The Hudson Valley Audubon Society of Westchester completed its 1999 hawk watch at Lenoir Preserve, which overlooks the Hudson River. The watch covered the period from August 26 through November 28. In 206 hours of field observation, members counted 5,365 raptors and 71,842 other migrating birds. The most numerous species were broad-winged hawks (1,680) and turkey vultures (1,277). Other noteworthy sightings included bald eagles (22), golden eagles (3), peregrine falcons (40), northern goshawks (11), and rough-legged hawk (1). *Joseph O'Connell, Ellen O'Connell, Michael Bochnik, Bill Van Wort*

Ice-bound Hudson River from Norrie State Park

by Esther Kiviat

Winter

December 1999

It is well to have some water in your neighborhood,
to give buoyancy to and float the earth.
Henry David Thoreau, *Walden*

12/1 Kowawese, HRM 59: It was 15°F at dawn and with a 15 mph wind, it felt like 25° below zero. I had to wonder as I watched the waves lap on the beach how there was no ice. The river temperature was a balmy 41°. By 1:00 PM the air had warmed to 25°. We hauled our seine through the shallows and caught a dozen spottail shiners, 3 white perch, and 1 small striped bass. One other fish was in the net. If it had not twitched, I would never have seen it. Wrapped in fallen oak leaves that came in with the net was a small brown bullhead catfish (67 mm). When it was time to leave, we tried stuffing the seine back into the basket in which it had come. No luck—the net was frozen. We tried to "fold" it. Besides not working, we looked pretty silly trying to fold an eighty-foot net. Then we hit on the answer. We dragged the seine back into the 41° water and the ice melted. We half-submerged the basket and loaded the net. *Tom Lake, Steve Stanne, Betsy Blair*

12/2 Danskammer Point, HRM 66.5: It was another early morning in the teens; skim ice crept out from the shore of the backwaters and creeks. A lone adult bald eagle was perched in a shoreline cottonwood just below Danskammer Point. The sun and the steam rising off the warm water outflow from the power plant bathed the bird in warmth. *Tom Lake*

Bald Eagles come in two flavors: adult and juvenile, male and female, mature and immature. The adult has a white head and tail, a dark brown body, and a yellow beak. A juvenile is brown all over (slightly lighter brown than the adult), normally has some white in its wing linings, and has a dark beak. Juveniles reach maturity in their fourth year. Some three-year-olds, on their way to their adult plumage, become "white extremes." Peter Dunne describes these *(Hawks in Flight*, 1988:147) as having immature plumage but also having a *white cape*. The **golden eagle**, seen infrequently along the Hudson, looks similar to the immature bald eagle but will have a "wash of gold" on its nape, white patches under its wings, and considerable white showing in its tail.

Immature bald eagle   by Wayne Kocher

Eagles
The bald eagle soars
through the sky of heaven and earth,
like the guardian of nature,
on the clouds giving birth.
Elizabeth Pacahuala, New Windsor School, NY

65

Upper Nyack, HRM 29: Yesterday I had to hammer an inch and a half of ice off the foredeck of my sailboat. Today the air was 48°F and the river 45°. A belted kingfisher flew so close that her red chest almost brushed my bow. The river looked green, milky yellow, and slow, as if it were going to sleep. *Daniel Wolff*

12/3 Moodna Creek, HRM 58: The ice was safe enough to walk about a hundred feet out from shore, at which point it began to sag. A good time to stop. Stretching out beyond was a thin veneer, strong enough for a drake mallard to sit upon, that eventually faded into cold, black water. *Tom Lake*

George's Island, HRM 39: I was at George's Island Park in the late afternoon to see if any wintering bald eagles were back. I heard some finch-like sounds and spotted three common redpolls. So far this had been a good year for winter finches with pine siskins, and now redpolls, making an appearance. *Larry Bickford*

The presence or absence of certain **"winter finches"** can often portend the coming winter. Cold, ice, and deep snow to the north can push crossbills, snow buntings, redpolls, evening grosbeaks, and pine siskins south. In mild winters, there are far fewer of these birds in the lower Hudson Valley.

12/4 Croton Point, HRM 34.5: Who knows what to make of this weather? Yesterday at Blue Mountain Reservation in Peekskill I heard a spring peeper; today at Croton Point Park I saw forsythia blooms. *Christopher Letts*

12/5 Farmer's Landing, HRM 67: The warm air and cold water had created an early morning fog; I could barely make out Cedarcliff 0.7 mile away across the river. It was 7:00 AM and I was looking for our wintering bald eagle pair to see if they had returned from Canada. The "eagle tree," a red oak on the side of Cedarcliff, was empty. However, higher up along the crest of the cliff, through the haze, I spotted a luminescent white head. An eagle was perched in a hardwood looking my way. And for a good reason. From somewhere behind me a second

adult flew out to the river's edge. No more than a hundred feet directly overhead, close enough to hear its wingbeats, it swung to the north and in a slow rhythmic fashion disappeared up Wappinger Creek. Like family visiting for the holidays, one of the joys of winter had occurred. Our eagle pair had returned. *Tom Lake*

Eagle at Croton Bay   by Wayne Kocher

Cedarcliff Wintering Bald Eagles
Return Date (first seen):

1999	1998	1997	1996	1995
12/5	12/25	12/13	12/31	12/21

"Eagle tree" means different things to different people. To famed eagle man *Charles Broley*, an eagle tree was any tree with an active nest. In the Hudson Valley it may mean a favored evening roost tree, daytime loafing tree, or feeding tree. Roost trees tend to be large white pines, oaks, cottonwoods, or others sheltered from the wind. Loafing trees, also large, tend to be more open to sunshine, while feeding trees are convenient to sources of potential food: usually open water where fish may be found. Wintering bald eagles often return daily to the same trees. *Jim Rod*

Croton Point, HRM 34: My first three winter eagles, all immatures, were soaring below the point today. *Larry Trachtenberg*

Hudson Valley **wintering Bald Eagles** leave their northern breeding territories during the late fall and early winter, as lakes and rivers there freeze over. They migrate south and begin to congregate on wintering grounds where open water foraging areas, daytime perches, and nighttime roosts are available and protected from human disturbance. Are their arrival dates predictable? It is likely that they are reflective of conditions in Canada. In a "hard winter," the bald eagle assemblage in the Hudson Valley may number fifty birds by midwinter. They come from diverse breeding areas and use the occasion to find mates and thus potentially deepen the gene pool. Although it is thought that they mate for life, there is some evidence that mismated pairs—not producing viable eggs—may eventually seek other partners.

12/8 Esopus Island 85: There was one adult bald eagle out on Esopus Island, a favorite hangout. We might have missed it except for the brilliant white head. *Fran Drakert, Bill Drakert*

Croton Point, HRM 34.5: Hours after I finished my early morning perambulation of the point I was still grinning. I had watched a merlin harass a red-tailed hawk, a kestrel hanging in the air over the landfill, and a peregrine stooping on a flock of starlings near the work barn. A falcon grand slam! Fresh coyote tracks were clearly printed in fresh mud—a first for me on this peninsula. And I've had my fourth sighting of a white-caped immature bald eagle, a so-called third-year white extreme. *Christopher Letts*

12/9 Sleepy Hollow, HRM 28: My class of *Irvington School* students was fascinated with the amount of water traffic we viewed today. From the bell deck of the Tarrytown Lighthouse we watched as the Coast Guard buoy tender *Red Beech* hoisted the huge channel buoy out and dropped in the smaller winter buoy. Tugs and pushboats from several companies passed and a giant oil tanker dwarfed them all. A huge barge housing a vast derrick nearly reached the underside of the central span of the Tappan Zee Bridge, 150' from the water to the underdeck. My interest was captured by the actions of a thirty-foot lobster boat with two men aboard. For the entire time we were on the bell deck they circled, grappled for a line on the bottom, then hauled in the train of rectangular eel pots fastened to the line. They seemed to be setting

their pots near the buoys, probably to make it easier to recover them. When we left the lighthouse the deck of the boat was piled six-feet-high with scores of pots. This was the sixth time this season I had watched them operate in broad daylight, easily seen from the shore and the Tappan Zee Bridge, and the fourth year in a row I've seen them eeling during October and November. *Christopher Letts*

There are special **American eel regulations** for the Hudson River. From the Battery to Troy and all tributaries upstream to the first barrier, eels 6"-14" only may be possessed, in any number, for bait. No eels greater than 14" may be possessed. No eels may be possessed for food.

Stony Kill with ice   by Esther Kiviat

12/10 Croton Point, HRM 34: The books say that the lovely cedar waxwings are "widespread but erratic" in winter. Here on Croton Point their movements seem much better organized. Sometime between the last week of October and the first week of December thousands of waxwings move steadily south and west to the tip of the Point and launch out for the western shore. Often, several thousand birds depart in a span of several days. This year's movement was more protracted. I did my counting during the first two hours of daylight, always covering the Point in the same way. Certainly I did not see every bird, and I missed a few days, but it gives an idea of the movement of waxwings that seems to me to be migratory. I will probably see waxwings there several times this winter but the flocks will be small and the birds will lack the sense of urgent purpose they show in November. For the fortnight past, I have not seen a single waxwing. The show is over for this year. I have never noted a corresponding movement in the spring of the year. *Christopher Letts*

Cedar Waxwing Migration:
Croton Point 1999

Date	Flocks	Birds	Date	Flocks	Birds
10/29	1	40	11/14	9	500
11/1	3	120	11/15	8	200
11/2	4	200	11/16	2	25
11/3	3	75	11/17	0	0
11/4	12	505	11/18	2	25
11/5	10	140	11/19	3	60
11/6	10	300	11/20	1	60
11/7	8	160	11/21	0	0
11/8	0	0	11/22	1	60
11/9	0	0	11/23	0	0
11/10	2	40	11/24	4	175

12/13 Newcomb, HRM 300: My husband and I are redoing an old house on the banks of the Hudson. We have a spectacular view looking right down the river with Vanderwacker Mountain as the backdrop. Just this morning I woke up and glanced outside and there, on the newly formed ice, was a river otter enjoying its morning catch. *Ruth Olbert*

Croton Point, HRM 34: It was a bright, sunny, breezy day, below freezing though I suspect much of that feeling came from the windchill. We were walking along the south beach at Croton Point and all along the way we kept hearing an incessant "tapping." Near a tidal rivulet leading to a small pond off the beach we found the source. It was a common flicker scurrying up and down a phragmites stem, tapping on the hollow reed, feeding on insects. *Martin Aronchick, Jacklin Aronchick, Russel Aronchick*

12/16 Ramshorn River, HRM 112.2: A late afternoon walk into the Ramshorn proved to be just the right thing to cure our early case of cabin (office) fever. To our surprise, we saw 40-50 robins during our half-mile walk. We wondered where they'd be a month from now? *Andy Turner, Anne Horst*

12/17 Poughkeepsie, HRM 75: At 5:00 PM, a half hour after sunset, a silver glow lingered over Blue Point. In its shadow, at least a thousand crows were perched in trees, shrubs, or in the air, along a hundred-meter stretch of Poughkeepsie shoreline. This was a new night roost that I had never seen before. *Tom Lake*

12/18 Cornwallville, HRM 124: The first flock of seven winter redpolls came to the feeders this morning. One looked different. It had a white rump and a speckled upper back—my first hoary redpoll. *Larry Biegel*

The **hoary redpoll** is a true "winter finch." They are an arctic breeder that rarely winters as far south as the Hudson Valley.

12/21 Poughkeepsie, HRM 75.5: A day before the solstice, the coming of winter, and I am warm inside of the Hudson River sloop *Clearwater* office. Every winter the staff sets up a humble tank of Hudson River fish to keep us connected to the river while tied to our winter office duties. The locals this year include an eel, spottail shiner, bluegill, and two brown bullheads. The two bullheads, each about four inches long, have become my favorites. Today as I fed them, I was struck by how shark-like they seemed to me. They work their heads, wiggling and thrashing their body under the rocks and bricks scattered along the tank bottom like reef sharks routing out prey. I watched one take a worm in its mouth and violently jerk its body back and forth like a mini-"Jaws" taking the bait. From above, their broad, flattened heads, splayed pectorals and fluid movements appear even more closely akin to their cartilaginous cousins. *Sean Madden*

Croton Point, HRM 34: We went to Croton Point to look for wintering bald eagles, remembering the thrill of seeing these massive birds last year. The river on the north side of the

68

Point was rough; the south was almost still. We could see a clear line in the river where the calm, sheltered water of Croton Bay met the broken river water west of the point. In the peaceful water a raft of ruddy ducks floated, stiff tails up and heads tucked in. We saw mallards, a female red-breasted merganser, and two ducks whose distinctive profiles identified them as canvasbacks. Two male buffleheads were diving and popping up. A kingfisher rattled, unseen. The phragmites along the beach were hopping and chittering with goldfinches—each bird a unique variation of brown, yellow, and white. An immature bald eagle flew low over our heads and we turned to follow its flight. By the railroad trestle we saw another bald eagle on an exposed log feeding, surrounded by circling gulls. Its head and tail were glowing white in the afternoon sun. Back up on the landfill we saw a female northern harrier ripping apart and swallowing a Norway rat: fur, bones, and tail. The hawk flew up and searched for more prey, slowly rocking from side to side, gliding close over the ground. She lowered her long legs, talons outstretched, and dropped onto another rat. She stood there a while, casually looking around as she squeezed it to death. Then she ate it. *Amy Silberkleit, Michael Shiffer, Isis Shiffer, Elijah Shiffer*

Manhattan, HRM 9: A young Cooper's hawk from the forests to the north today paid a visit to Riverbank State Park's 28 acres of playing fields, picnic areas, and sidewalks atop the North River Sewage Treatment Plant. The accipiter swept low along the railing overlooking the Hudson, probably hoping to ambush an unwary house sparrow or starling. Unsuccessful, it spread its wings and tail to catch the blustery northwest breeze, rose upwards, and soared off to the east, where a local red-tailed hawk was already hanging high and kite-like in the sky. *Steve Stanne, Chuck Keene, Dick Kearns*

12/22 Fort Miller, HRM 192.5: Canada geese dominated the river today, though in lesser numbers than recently. The island before me, about sixty feet offshore, splits the river's

current, drawing ducks and herons to its fruitful shallows. Just as I was folding my spotting scope, seven snow geese came in low immediately before me. Four of them were white and, to my surprise, three were blue morphs, one of which was immature in featureless dark feathering. It was a surprisingly large bird, but I suspect that its heavy feathering projected such an appearance. *Jim Sotis*

The **blue goose** is a gray version of the white snow goose. It is the same species, just a blue/gray color phase (see Peterson, 1980:44).

Poughkeepsie, HRM 75.5: From Waryas Riverfront Park I scanned the railroad bridge, which spans the Hudson at Poughkeepsie, with binoculars and a spotting scope. I saw a pair of peregrine falcons on a bridge abutment feeding on a kill. *Chester Vincent*

Chelsea, HRM 65.2: It was an hour before sunrise and the sky was still dark gray. Light snow filtered down through a stand of ailanthus (tree-of-heaven) carpeting the shoreline and hanging in the elbows of trees. It was the first dawn of winter, a mild one at that. The air was barely below freezing and the river was wide open—no ice in sight. Across the river at Danskammer Point a pair of adult bald eagles were perched in a riverside red maple, keeping close watch for a fish to drift past or a duck to get careless. *Tom Lake*

Croton Point, HRM 34.5: This was a once-in-a-lifetime occasion—every 69 years to be exact—a full moon on the Winter's Solstice. Thirty of us, lunatics all, gathered at sunset atop the Croton landfill to bid winter welcome and take in the sights. This was also going to be a lunar perigee, when the moon would be as close to earth as it gets all year, about 222,000 miles. At 4:30 PM the ebb tide went slack in Croton Bay and the sun set over the Rockland County hills in a splash of pink and red and purple. The moon would have popped up in the east just twenty minutes later if we were on a coastal horizon. However, the spectacle was delayed about 15 minutes before it slowly appeared over the Ossining hills with a soft orange glow. Our group let out a collective gasp. Jupiter shone brightly overhead along with a much dimmer Saturn. We shared hot cider, toasted marshmallows, and basked in the glow of a big old friendly moon. *Christopher Letts, Nancy Letts, Andra Sramek, Joe Dunn, Elijah Shiffer, Amy Silberkleit, Isis Shiffer, Tom Lake*

12/24 Farmer's Landing, HRM 67: At dawn of Christmas Eve day the air was 15°F. Black ice was creeping out from the shoreline of Wappinger Creek and overnight flurries had whitened the earth. On the chance that we'd see an eagle, we went to the terrace at Farmer's Landing, a hundred feet over the river. With binoculars we scanned the shoreline from Chelsea to New Hamburg and from Roseton to Milton—a six mile view—without seeing an eagle. Frozen to the bone we hurried back into our warm car and slowly drove away on Old Troy Road, a narrow oneway passage high on a bluff over the south side of Wappinger Creek. We had not traveled 150' before I spotted a scruffy white head. We slowed to a stop, rolled down the windows, and watched an adult bald eagle perched on the limb of a hillside red oak. The eagle, I guessed a female by her size, was not more than 75' away. As long as we stayed in the car, even with the engine and our mouths running, the eagle continued to perch on that limb. Its back was to us and her head would swivel around every few seconds like a contortionist as she kept an eye on us—a penetrating stare. I also guessed that this was the female of the "Cedarcliff pair" that has been part of our winter for five years. Within a minute or two we moved on and left her to the task of creek-watching. *Susanne Lake, Phyllis Lake, Tom Lake*

Bald eagle viewing, when practical, is almost always more successful from inside a vehicle. Their eyesight is exceptional, often said to be 3-4 times as acute as that of humans. Soaring eagles may be able to spot each other at distances of up to 65 kilometers. Eagle expert *Pete Nye* estimates that the "alert distance" of an eagle is 250 meters and that the "flight distance" is 125 meters. That is, basically, how close they will let you get without taking off. However, if you are part of a vehicle, eagles seem unable to sense that

you are human. Professional photographer *Wayne Kocher* has taken some remarkable photos of eagles using a car window mount for his 35 mm SLR camera.

Farmer's Landing, HRM 67: By midafternoon the air temperature had risen to 32°F and we repeated our early morning route. We found a second bald eagle perched on a different oak limb, not more than a hundred feet from our car window. This eagle was a little smaller and I guessed it was a male. Even though we stayed inside our car the eagle was fidgeting around on the limb and appeared ready to leave. The white head and tail told us it was an adult, but as it dropped down off the limb, wheeled and banked across in front of us, we saw that it had a feathered "white cape" on its back, nearly connecting the white head with the tail. This was probably a three-year-old "white extreme." It righted its course, exited Wappinger Creek over the train trestle, and slowly made its way across the river to the day perches at Cedarcliff. *Tom Lake, Phyllis Lake*

What is the greatest threat to wintering bald eagles? The single highest cause of mortality, among wintering bald eagles in the Hudson Valley, is high speed trains. At least six have been killed in the last four years. Trains inadvertently kill animals that are crossing the tracks to reach the river, most commonly opossum, raccoons, woodchucks, and white-tailed deer. Scavengers such as crows, fox, and coyote find these carcasses to be an easy meal. Wintering eagles soaring overhead find the dead deer between the rails just as inviting. They set down to feed, get engrossed in the meal, and never hear the train approaching. *Pete Nye*

12/26 Croton River, HRM 34: The first of the winter series of eagle watches was scheduled for today, but warm weather and a lack of snow seems to have delayed their customary arrival from northern lands by several weeks. It was with relief and pleasure that I spotted a mature eagle perched in a streamside tree. Another bird, an immature, swept in from a cottonwood perch at the base of Croton Point. This was the bird I have dubbed "Capeman" for the extensive white on its back that identifies it as a three-year-old, a "white extreme." Capeman hovered about twenty feet above the surface of the water, then dropped to about six feet off the water to join yet another immature eagle, likewise hovering. The hovering went on for a good 45 seconds, with the two birds jockeying and feinting at each other, but remaining focused on the clear fast waters of the Croton River. Finally a drake common merganser burst from the water right beneath the birds. Both eagles stooped, both missed, and a very lucky merganser disappeared under the railroad bridge. My impression was that the eagles had gotten in each other's way. Capeman returned to the cottonwood and the other eagle perched near the adult on the riverbank. Neither attempted to pursue the merganser. A short time later I spotted another adult eagle soaring over George's Island, five miles upriver, the first eagle sighting I had there this season. If my group doesn't get to see an eagle today, at least I will have a good story for them. *Christopher Letts*

12/28 Riparius, HRM 251: There is a wonderful boggy pond on a tributary of the Hudson about a quarter-mile from Riparius in Warren County. In a good year it has a population of about 150 plants of swamp pink. The area is owned by a logger. These need to be protected, but no one seems interested. *Evelyn Greene*

Cedarcliff, HRM 67.5: Our bald eagle pair was perched along the top of the ridge, a bit further back into the stand of hardwoods than usual, sheltered from a bitter cold biting northwest wind. Seconds after I found them in the binoculars, one flared out over the ridge, turned, spread its wings, and soared across the cliff face. *Susanne Lake, Phyllis Lake*

Bald Eagle field identification
1. Eagles soar on flat wings, unlike vultures, osprey, and harriers which have a dihedral angle of varying degrees in the fixing of their wings.
2. They soar on wings the size of ironing boards.
3. Bald eagles could be confused, albeit briefly, with adult greater black-backed gulls, particularly at a distance.
4. As they perch along the river, their posture has a regal countenance.

12/30 Ashokan Reservoir, HRM 91: At this Esopus Creek impoundment we saw bluebirds—the last of the millennium for us. *Fran Drakert, Bill Drakert*

Adult bald eagle   by Wayne Kocher

George's Island, HRM 39: Off in the distance we saw a large brown raptor soaring on flat wings. Was this an immature bald eagle? Then an audible cry came back to us on the wind, *"K-I-R-R-R-R."* It was a red-tailed hawk! *Andra Sramek, Christopher Letts, Tom Lake*

12/31 Hoosic River, HRM 172: It was a clear, brisk morning, three miles up the Hoosic from the Hudson, with the river running strong shore to shore. A dozen common mergansers, held together in a tight raft, floating leisurely in the fast current. *Joan Sheppard* had just come back from a walk downriver where she had checked on a small cluster of mallards. As I picked up my spotting scope, I was startled by the sudden appearance of a string of ten white-winged scoters flying directly above me. Evidently they had been following the Hoosic, heading for the Hudson. We followed their flight until they were lost to viewing behind the screen of wooded cover. It was a wonderful accent to wildness to which we were sole witness. *Jim Sotis*

White-winged scoters are uncommon visitors to the Hudson Valley. They are seen in migration or as the result of being blown offcourse by a nor'easter. These black sea ducks have white wing patches and a knobby orange bill. Scoters breed inland in Canada and winter along the Atlantic Coast from Labrador to the Southeastern U.S.

Farmer's Landing, HRM 67: Was this a sundown on the millennium? As daylight dimmed, we spotted the Cedarcliff bald eagle pair across the river, perched in the treeline high on the cliff face. Before long they were reduced to two fuzzy white dots, and then darkness. *Tom Lake, Phyllis Lake*

Hudson Valley: If you believe that a decade can culminate in a year that ends with 9, then this was, nationally, the warmest decade ever recorded by the *National Weather Service*.

Winterscape
The water is frozen solid with glistening ice and snow,
The ground is white and slippery like anyone should know.
The hovering trees are tall which gently sway back and forth,
And snow is gently landing, probably toward the north.
Sharonrose Pulliam, New Windsor School, NY

January 2000

How do you expect the birds to sing
when their groves are cut down?
Henry David Thoreau, *Walden*

1/1 Farmer's Landing, HRM 67: 12:15 A.M. Fireworks could be seen upriver and downriver as the Hudson Valley celebrated the new year (but perhaps not a new millennium). The lights of the valley were lit and the power generating facility at Danskammer hummed. As a counterpoint to the human festivities, the timeless belt of *Orion* hung overhead in the starry night sky. On the Hunter's shoulder was *Betelgeuse* ("Beetle Juice"), a bright star, yet 500 million light years away. It offered some perspective to our celebration of 1999 years. A small flock of Canada geese could be heard but not seen honking their way in the darkness from the river inland. *Tom Lake*

Somewhere along the way, one of our **millennia** will have to last for a thousand years. If this night was the first of a *new* millennium, then the *old* one had lasted only 999 years.

Ulster Park, HRM 88: A Carolina wren was singing for *Fran Drakert* on her early morning dog walk: *"Tea kettle, tea kettle tea kettle tea."* Later I spotted a bluebird; any day you see a bluebird can't be all bad and I wondered if that applied to a new millennium. *Bill Drakert*

Farmer's Landing, HRM 67: It was a frosty dawn, the first of new year, and we found our bald eagle pair sharing an oak limb on the south side of Wappinger Creek. From our idling auto we stopped not 75' away, and wished them a Happy New Year. *Phyllis Lake, Tom Lake*

Highland Falls, HRM 48.5: We had just come home after a New Year's Eve celebration at the new Rose Center for Earth and Space at the American Museum of Natural History in Manhattan. We were greeted by a magnificent adult bald eagle perched on a white oak branch just in front of our porch overlooking the

Hudson River—a wonderful way to start the new millennium. *Connie Eristoff, Anne P. Sidamon-Eristoff*

Round Island, HRM 45: An adult bald eagle, first spotted three hours earlier and three miles downriver at Jones Point, seemed to be following us, soaring along the river to Iona Island. At 2:00 PM, a different eagle was seen perched in a tall tree on Round Island. *Tom Fitzpatrick* identified this one as a golden eagle. *Bobbi Buske, Ed Lenik*

Mute swan   by Tom Lake

Croton Point, HRM 34: This was our 15th annual New Year's Day hike and ciderfest. A very unwinter-like south breeze and air temperatures in the 40°s made it feel like late autumn. We spotted a pair of buffleheads on Croton Bay and an immature bald eagle eying them from a marshside cottonwood, but little else. It would take a winter storm to lure the winter migrants south. *Mike Bannan, Kathleen Peterson, Christopher Letts, Andra Sramek, Barry Keegan, Tom Lake*

Anthony's Nose, HRM 46: Air temperature was in the 50°s as we hiked up the trail. The fog cleared as we came to our first spectacular view of the Hudson and Iona Island. To the south we watched an immature bald eagle soar over the river and into the trees of Dunderberg Mountain. We flushed a hawk from a high branch. As it passed above us, its size, brown-flecked chest and white underwings and belly identified it as a young red-shouldered hawk. Further up the trail, we watched a red-tailed hawk take flight from a treetop. *Michael Shiffer, Amy Silberkleit, Isis Shiffer, Elijah Shiffer*

Alpine, NJ, HRM 18: We were hiking the Shore Trail under the Palisades a quarter-mile south of the Alpine Boat basin when we spotted a large number of canvasbacks out on the river The raft of canvasbacks, 106 ducks, was spread out in a long line, just floating in place in the ebb slack tide. On the edge was a lone male bufflehead, six mallards, and two female red-breasted mergansers. *Bob Rancan, Nancy Slowik*

1/3 LaGrange, HRM 75: An unseasonably mild air flow from the south combined with a storm track to our west to allow record breaking warmth to prevail over the Hudson Valley. It was 60°F in the Town of Poughkeepsie. *Gene Martin*

Manhattan, HRM 5: A record high air temperature for the date of 64°F was recorded today. *National Weather Service*

1/4 Town of Wappinger, HRM 68: Despite an overcast sky and a light drizzle, the air was an April-like 65°F. This was a record high temperature for the date. *National Weather Service*

American coot   by Wayne Kocher

Newark, NJ: A record high air temperature for the date of 65°F was recorded today.

1/7 Staatsburg, HRM 87: As I watched a large raft of canvasbacks out on the river in front of the Mills Mansion, an adult bald eagle flew past heading up the river. *Bill Drakert*

1/8 Highland Falls, HRM 48.5: We watched a beautiful immature bald eagle perched on the same white oak branch outside our porch that had held an adult bald eagle a week earlier. It surveyed Con Hook Marsh and the Hudson River. *Connie Eristoff, Anne P. Sidamon-Eristoff*

1/10 Poughkeepsie, HRM 75: As estimated seven to ten thousand crows were roosting nightly along the river at Poughkeepsie (see December 17). I have seen them there since November. They arrive just before sunset, first from the northwest, then the west, and finally the southwest, from across the river, and in a half hour they are all roosted. It reminded me of Alfred Hitchcock's movie "The Birds." *Vincent Francese, Lydia Francese*

Wappinger Creek, HRM 67.5: First light came late with drizzle, fog, and an air temperature of 42°F. It was low tide in the creek and the first quarter-mile of tidewater was covered, nearly bank to bank, with Canada geese—a thousand birds. Common mergansers, mallards, mute swans, and one great blue heron vied for position among the geese. Within an hour they began to lift off, in groups of 50, 75, 100, as though they had drawn lots overnight. Even in the low ceiling I could make out their Vs as they headed south. *Tom Lake*

1/11 Hudson Valley, HRM 68-45: Each January, the NYSDEC Endangered Species Unit conducts a midwinter bald eagle survey of wintering bald eagles in New York State. The following observations were typical of a one-day search for eagles along a 23-mile reach of the river. *Tom Lake*

Farmer's Landing, HRM 67: My tally for the day quickly became three, when I spotted the "Cedarcliff pair" perched side-by-side across the river on Soap Hill. A third adult was perched in a shoreline tree a quarter mile downriver at Danskammer Point. As I left this viewing spot to head downriver I passed a fourth adult perched on the south side of Old Troy Road along Wappinger Creek. I almost missed eagle number five. It was an immature bird that had blended into the scenery despite the fact that it was watching me from only 150' away. Even though I stayed behind the wheel of my truck so I would not scare them, they took off and flew downriver to Danskammer Point. One of the tricks to accurately counting eagles is to know where your birds are going so you don't count one twice.

Newburgh, HRM 62-59: One of the winter certainties is that there will always be an adult bald eagle perched in a hardwood tree right at the tip of Denning Point at the outflow of Fishkill Creek. At least it seems that way. Eagle number six was there this morning. Scanning the eastern shoreline to the south produced number seven, an adult, in the crown of a sycamore. A near-certainty of winter is that there will be an adult perched along Cornwall Bay waiting for the tide to ebb and reveal its richness of fishes. There I saw number eight.

Iona Island, HRM 46-44: My final stop for the morning was the Route 6/202 pulloff on the east side of the river just below the Bear

Mountain Bridge. From this vantage you have a two-mile view from Bear Mountain south to Dunderberg Mountain. Another important aspect of searching for bald eagles is knowing where to look. They are not everywhere and, after a while, it becomes apparent that certain trees will hold birds when other do not. Eagles favor perches with a view. There is a small grove of white pine on Iona Island that will hold eagles if there are any around. Today there were two adults, numbers nine and ten. *Tom Lake*

Annual NYSDEC Mid-Winter Bald Eagle Survey (ground only) for HRM 68-44

	Adult	Immature	Total	Air
1999	13	3	16	12°F
2000	9	1	10	42°F

Waterford, HRM 159: It was a strange sight. The water had been drained from the Erie Canal for the winter. That, in itself, was not strange. It happens every winter. However, we had conducted research on the fish populations at this end of Mohawk River from June through November, in water up to our noses. Now it was all gone; all the fish were gone as well. In August we had captured a tiny brindled madtom, a very uncommon catfish, along the shore at Lock 3. Now there were only a few puddles that would freeze solid in a week. All else was dry ground. The thousands of fish we saw all summer were gone. Each spring when the Erie Canal locks open, a full community of fish fauna is drawn in from the Hudson River to the east and the Mohawk River to the west. *Tom Lake, Bob Schmidt*

Cohoes, HRM 157: The falls at Cohoes roared as the water poured out of the Mohawk River. A few days of rain had produced a torrent of whitewater. A thousand gulls, mostly greater black-backed gulls, wheeled in circles in the mist below the falls. Just above the falls, an immature bald eagle watched from a perch in the top of a hardwood. *Tom Lake*

Eagle watching at China Pier   by Tom Lake

Farmer's Landing, HRM 67: *Craig O'Donnell* spotted 20 bald eagles (8 adults, 12 immatures) along the river in the mile and a half between Danskammer and Cedarcliff. Nine had gathered along the river at Danskammer; another eleven were clustered around Cedarcliff.

1/12   New Hamburg, HRM 67.5: After two days of strong north winds the ebb tide just drained the shoreline. From out in front of our home, we could see acres of mudflats, rarely exposed. Wappinger Creek, a robust tidal tributary a half-mile to the south, was reduced to a trickle. *Sue Clifford*

1/13   New Hamburg, HRM 67: Winter arrived today with a vengeance. By first light flurries were falling in the Mid-Hudson Valley and by dusk there was six inches of snow on the ground. Waterfowl, geese and ducks, that had settled in Wappinger Creek, appeared as hummocks of snow. *Tom Lake*

1/14   New Hamburg, HRM 67: Air temperatures overnight fell to -5°F with a windchill of -34°. At dawn Wappinger Creek was frozen over. Groups of mallards seemed fixed in the ice but had managed to maintain narrow slots of open water by paddling. *Tom Lake*

Croton Bay, HRM 34: On the coldest day this winter we went to the south shore of Croton Point at low tide. Out of the wind it was noticeably warmer. Ice coated the rocks, bricks, and sand. Three females and one male common merganser were swimming in the sunlight. An immature bald eagle was perched in a hardwood by the shore and when it lifted off we noticed a broad streak of white down the middle of its back. It swooped straight for one of the female mergansers, dropped its legs, talons extended. The merganser shot straight out of the water with a huge splash. The eagle, having missed, veered off to the opposite shore. *Michael Shiffer, Amy Silberkleit, Isis Shiffer, Elijah Shiffer*

1/15   Farmer's Landing, HRM 67: There was ice on the river. It was like someone had turned on a switch. Several hundred Canada geese paddled in the sparse open water as a pair of immature eagles stood along the edge of the ice. If they were this year's fledglings, this would be their first ice. What perplexing thoughts might be going through their heads? They took off together, wheeling, circling, interacting, much like siblings. A pair of adults was perched across the river on Soap Hill. Another pair was out getting a ride on the ice off Danskammer Point. It was the first ice of winter and the birds had all come out to play. *Margaret Lake, Tom Lake*

Fishkill Ridge, HRM 61.4: As we entered the woods above Beacon, two red-tailed hawks exited, calling and circling together. We followed Dry Brook up through a forest of hemlocks to Fishkill Ridge where mountain laurel and blueberry bushes grew among the stunted pitch pine and scrub oak. Below us was the Hudson and a 17-mile view from Cornwall to Poughkeepsie. We descended through a mixed hardwood forest following a wandering line of bobcat tracks in the snow. *Amy Silberkleit, Michael Shiffer, Isis Shiffer, Elijah Shiffer*

Hudson Valley: We were finally able to fly and make the 21st annual Mid-Winter Bald Eagle Count. From Albany to the Tappan Zee we spotted 28 bald eagles, compared to 14 in 1999. In southeast New York State (combined Hudson and Delaware systems) we counted a record 238 eagles (119 adults, 119 immatures). We had seen only 179 birds in 1999. Bald eagle populations in general are increasing throughout eastern North America, including states adjacent to New York. *Pete Nye*

While landbound observers were able to do their **Mid-Winter Bald Eagle Count** on January 10, the weather had conspired to keep the NYSDEC spotter aircraft on the ground until today.

1/16   Wappinger Creek, HRM 67.5: The bitter cold may be driving eagles downriver to find open water. In early afternoon I spotted an immature eagle being closely pursued by a flock of determined crows across the mouth of Wappinger Creek. *Gene Martin*

1/17   New Hamburg, HRM 67.5: In the face of a brutally cold north wind, I checked the hills across the river with binoculars. In the swale between Cedarcliff and Soap Hill, 4 immature and 4 adult bald eagles were hunkered down, back in the trees, out of the wind. *Craig Thompson*

Wappinger Creek, HRM 67.5: It was still ninety minutes to low water yet the level of the tidal Wappinger was the lowest I had ever seen. My five-year-old grandson, *Alfred Francese*, recognized it and asked where the creek had gone. The frozen watershed and a strong north wind had combined to blow the water out of the creek. *Vincent Francese*

Manhattan, HRM 5: At just 8°F, today was the coldest day in New York City in three years. *National Weather Service*

1/18   Red Hook, HRM 97: Precisely at dawn we recorded an air temperature of -8°F. *National Weather Service*

Poughkeepsie, HRM 75: A strong pressure gradient between an outgoing ocean storm and a strong ridge of high pressure combined to produce windchills in excess of -40°F. *Gene Martin*

Town of Wappinger, HRM 67: At first light a Cooper's Hawk came barreling through our backyard near the river scattering goldfinches, house finches, juncos, white-throats, cardinals, and my golden retriever. We had heard a flicker call loudly a few seconds earlier and we wondered if there was a connection. The Cooper's perched in a tree 55' from our back window and we got a good three-minute look with our binoculars: "Bird TV," we like to call it. *Phyllis Lake, Tom Lake*

Manhattan, HRM 5: This was the coldest morning in Manhattan since 1994. *National Weather Service*

1/19   Farmer's Landing, HRM 67: Dawn felt like a veritable heat wave. At 3°F, a windchill of -11°, the ice on the lenses of my binoculars and the chill against my face were manageable. Our eagles were hiding, or celebrating. *Tom Lake*

1/21   Farmer's Landing, HRM 67: At first light, a biting cold northwest wind made it feel like -10°F. The full moon was setting in the west. An overnight total lunar eclipse had been obscured by cloud cover. A week of true winter weather, eight days of deep-freeze, and the river was bank-to-bank ice. With three inches of fresh snow on top it looked like the salt flats of Death Valley. It was one of those rare winter days when it appeared that I could snowshoe right across the Hudson on the ice—there were no obvious open leads between me and Cedarcliff, three-quarters of a mile away. Large irregular blocks, stacked one upon another, were strewn across the white expanse. A large raptor came flapping down the river near the eastern shore. It was a female northern harrier heading south looking very much out of place against the frozen winter riverscape. Harriers, or marsh hawks, depend primarily on the open water of tidemarshes and this one would not find any for at least another forty miles. *Tom Lake*

A **"lead"** is an opening in the ice. In the arctic ice pack, a lead means life or death for whales and other marine mammals who must surface for air. On Hudson River tidewater, a lead can be transitory, appearing for a few minutes only to be closed by ice floes pushed by the current. In a cold winter, open water leads are important for waterfowl, providing room to set down. For diving ducks it's an opportunity to feed. By extension, open water leads are important for bald eagles as well, with fish and waterfowl being their primary prey items.

1/22   China Pier, HRM 43: It was the ninth day in a row of sub-freezing air temperatures. The southern gateway to the Hudson Highlands was an ice conveyor; huge floes more than a foot thick and the size of city blocks were drifting downriver in the current. Three adult and three immature bald eagles had taken up temporary residence out on the ice, getting a free ride in search of dinner. Between Bear Mountain and the Croton River (HRM 46-34), *Wayne Kocher and Chris Kocher* reported seeing 15 eagles, one of which may have been a golden eagle. *Tom Lake*

River of Ice
The river lay motionless,
In a blanket of snow and ice.
Where harbor seals lay lazily,
And where eagles hunt for fish.
Soon the snow and ice will melt,
And the river will wake up.
Spring will have come,
And there will be new life.
Jason Baldwin, New Windsor School, NY

Ulster Park, HRM 88: To the west the snow-covered Catskills looked beautiful. To the east the river was well frozen. I guess the Coast Guard icebreakers will be earning their keep for a while. Along River Road I spotted an adult bald eagle perched riverside. *Bill Drakert*

1/23   New Hamburg, HRM 67.5: Walking along Point Street to the river I was able to spot seven eagles in the air, out on the ice, or perched across the river at Cedarcliff. I had counted six others a few minutes earlier north of Cedarcliff near the dolomite quarry, bringing the total to 13 bald eagles (3 adults, 10 immatures). *Rich Buckey*

1/24   Hoosic River, HRM 172: It was another of those mornings when the lower Hoosic River—three miles from the Hudson—inspired a sense of pure wildness, so transforming the experience, which never fails to linger. I was drawn to an emerging distant sight in the sky upriver. At first it appeared as a massive, floating, seamless apparition spread in depth and width, stretching back beyond viewing. An incredible flight of at least two thousand Canada geese stretched across the horizon. By the hundreds they kept their formation until descending, exuding enormous energy, gabbling with a ringing resonance as they side-slipped to splash down and literally blanket a great stretch of the river. I now estimated their number to be 2,500-3,000. Open water ended about 300 yards downriver. An ice sheet dominated the remaining run of the Hoosic to its merger with the Hudson just beyond the Lock 4 exit. I remained for a while, taken with all that energy exuding from that wondrous scene. Suddenly, flying in from upriver came a northern goshawk, the greatest of our accipiters, steadily pumping its wings flying directly before me over the massive blanket of geese. *Jim Sotis*

Farmer's Landing, HRM 67: Today was the first day in twelve that the air temperature reached 32°F; at midday it felt warm at 33°. The surface of the river looked like a moonscape; only through movement of the massive blocks of ice in the current could you discern that it was a river and not a glacial valley. *Tom Lake*

1/25   Hudson Valley: An unexpected turn to the west by a classic nor'easter brought a surprise snowstorm to the Hudson Valley with snow totals to twelve inches. Intense snowfall and winds to 30 mph at the outset gave us blizzard-like conditions. The storm's center came so close that we spent much of the time in the "dry slot" of the storm, sparing us from a crippling blizzard. *Gene Martin*

1/26 Wappinger Creek, HRM 69: At 8:30 AM, I drove across the creek near the Dutchess County Airport. Just beyond the bridge I spotted an adult bald eagle perched on a branch looking upstream. I stopped the car and the eagle turned its head in my direction. We locked eyes. I was surprised and excited. *Stephen Wilanewicz*

New Hamburg, HRM 67.5: The mid-Hudson Valley was emerging from a foot of snow that had fallen over the previous 24 hours. Except when the current inched the ice along, you could imagine that it was 17,000 years ago, and this was a great glacier wedged between the uplands. From out of the low light of a weak dawn came three snow geese, heading downriver only 150' overhead. I was surprised by their presence—totally unexpected. They filled my binoculars and appeared very purposeful in their mad dash south to find open water or an open cornfield. Ten minutes later, while I was watching a pair of adult bald eagles across the way at Cedarcliff, I heard the *"Honk, honk, honk"* of Canada geese. Heading downriver, about halfway across and several hundred feet in the air, was a huge V of Canadas, easily more than a hundred birds. *Tom Lake*

1/27 Croton River, HRM 34: "Seven Eagles and a White Perch." For fifteen minutes I watched seven immature bald eagles swoop and soar. One bird always carried the perch in its talons and the others were in hot pursuit. The fish was dropped to the ice when the chase got too close; all would dive for it and then it was another bird's turn to be "it." The story was recounted to Metro North employees who said they had witnessed similar interactions. In the past, eagles have been observed in this behavior using sticks, clams, and even chunks of ice. *Christopher Letts*

Eagle Games! The interaction between eagles is always a fascinating thing to watch. When it is between adults, we can surmise that it is courtship behavior. When it is between immature birds, we wonder if it is play. A mix of adults and immatures and we think of parents and children. All of these interpretations may seem anthropomorphic, but it is the only analogy we have. The range of "games" seems to grow each winter. One of the more common is a game of "tag," where one eagle will carry a stick, a fish, an oyster shell, even a chunk of ice, and the others will pursue. When the prize is finally dropped, another eagle picks it up in their talons and the pursuit is renewed.

Croton Point, HRM 34: An immature eagle left the roosting tree on the south shore of the point as we stepped from the snow onto the ice. Its white chest and the white blaze on its back identified the bird as one we had seen before. We were surprised to see an adult red-tailed hawk remaining in the same tree close to where the eagle had been. As we enjoyed sliding on the thick ice, two eagles engaged in a game of "pass the rock." One bird, dark with a white tail, clutched a rock in its talons and circled with an adult eagle, turning in the air, legs extended. The rock landed on the ice and was retrieved by the immature bird who dropped it down again and picked it up several times before joining the adult who was flying toward the Croton River train trestle. We could see three more immature eagles on the ice by the edge of the open water. Another adult was competing with an immature for a good perch on a large snag sticking out of the bay. From the south side of the point we spotted a pair of northern harriers, the larger brown female and the smaller gray and white male. They skimmed over the phragmites, out of the wind, searching for prey. *Michael Shiffer, Isis Shiffer, Amy Shiffer, Amy Silberkleit*

1/28 Newburgh, HRM 60: Some ice on the river in winter is a good thing. But this was becoming too much of a good thing for eagles and waterfowl. With air temperatures in the single digits, windchills to -30°F, there was too much ice on the river. Coast Guard tug 109 had cut a path downriver in the channel. However, the resulting few open leads held nothing more than a few gulls. Along the 25 miles from Poughkeepsie to West Point, the river was choked, bank to bank, with ice. Solid shelves reached out from the shore to the channel, where it was a river of ice, of tightly-packed floes, barely creeping along in the current. In early morning nary an eagle was to be seen. The wintering eagles were here for open water and the weather had turned the Mid-Hudson reach into an arctic sea. *Tom Lake*

Dutchess Junction, HRM 59: In late afternoon, observations were coming in pairs along the Hudson on Route 9D: A pair of red-tailed hawks flew low over the road ahead of me. Each had a gray squirrel gripped in its talons. A mile up the road a pair of red fox scampered across in front of me and disappeared into the woods. *Andra Sramek*

Croton Bay, HRM 34: By midmorning, 17 bald eagles (2 adults, 15 immatures) had assembled on the ice of Croton Bay. *Oren Smith*

Alpine, NJ, HRM 18: It was a very cold (8°F) and windy morning. From the north end of Picture Point, on the Palisades, we spotted several raptors flying over the Hudson. One was an adult peregrine falcon flying over the large ice floes in the river. It was followed by a dark phase rough-legged hawk and an adult red-tailed hawk. Along the Palisades we also saw three turkey vultures. *Nancy Slowik, Sandy Bonardi*

1/29 Santanoni Preserve, HRM 300: I was back at Santanoni Preserve near Newcomb in the High Peaks of the Adirondacks to complete a five-mile trek to Newcomb Lake. Two days ago, after the first major snowfall of 2000, I had skied one mile in from the gate to the farm at Santanoni where I met *Ruth Allen* of Newcomb. It was 7°F with high winds, the kind that atomizes the fresh, dry snow back into the air and diffuses the brilliant sun to a dim smudge. Still, it was a beautiful, sunny day with mountainous visibility in the 75-100 mile range. Today I finished the last four miles plus an extra mile onto the middle of the frozen lake as daylight turned to twilight and then darkness

under a spectacular and dazzling winter sky. *Sirius,* the Dog Star and brightest of all in the sky, blazed with intense color in the east below *Orion.* Jupiter filled *Pisces* high in the south as *Altair* twinkled in the west. Above all there was silence. Natural silence has become one of the rarest of all natural wonders, and one of the dearest in the noisy world. When I finally managed to get truly still and quiet, my own screeching contact with the cold, hard snow, ah what a bliss. As an old Zen proverb says, "Walk in the dark, In your best clothes." Amen. *Doug Reed*

New Hamburg, HRM 68: It was a sunny day and we decided to take a quick trip to the river in hopes of seeing bald eagles. At the train station we spotted three eagles out on the ice. At the New Hamburg Yacht Club we spotted three more, one adult, two immatures, sitting on different ice floes out in the channel (there was a lot of ice and not much open water). At White's Marina we found 14 common mergansers and 4 more bald eagles across the river perched in trees just above Danskammer Point. *Allan Michelin, Barbara Michelin*

Croton Reservoir, HRM 34: What a day for watching bald eagles! From our home on the Croton River we watched two adults and one immature soar and dive from 500' toward the Croton Reservoir. By late afternoon we spotted 14 bald eagles (4 adults, 10 immatures) out on the ice, a half-mile east of the dam. None appeared to be feeding although, a while later, two immatures made a weak pass at a small raft of black ducks that were in nearby open water. *Robert Pearson Jr.*

Sleepy Hollow, HRM 28: The three miles of river ahead of us were seemingly an unbroken expanse of ice from the North Tarrytown Lighthouse across to Nyack in Rockland County. The Coast Guard vessel, *Hawser,* wove an ice-breaking pattern across the Tappan Zee. It was an effort to keep drifting ice floes from forming larger rafts that would impede river traffic. *Andra Sramek, Christopher Letts, Tom Lake*

1/30 Farmer's Landing, HRM 67: At first light the air temperature was -6°F. The river ice was growing. As with each of the previous five days, no eagles could be seen. It appeared that they were flying south each morning before I arrived, finding open water and forage, and then returning to their night roosts in the late afternoon. *Tom Lake*

Highland Falls, HRM 48.5: Today we saw two adults and one immature bald eagle flying up and down the riverbank at Con Hook Marsh looking for prey. At times it seemed as though the adults were trying the chase the immature bird away. *Connie Eristoff, Anne P. Sidamon-Eristoff*

Ice Fishing at Whoopie Lake   by Martin Aronchick

Montrose, HRM 39: At noon, our group of a dozen ice-fishers walked the perimeter of Whoopie Lake in George's Island Park. Overhead a pair of red-tailed hawks, soaring in ever-shrinking circles, engaged in play with talon-grabs and wing-touches. Nearly ten inches of ice covered the lake with a cap of new snow that had fallen overnight. We followed coyote tracks in the snow and concluded that this animal had been walking slowly, as were we, around the edge of the lake. The coyote had been searching for mice and voles; we were heading back to our bonfire to toast a few more marshmallows. *Martin Aronchick, Russel Aronchick, Elijah Shiffer, Isis Shiffer, Michael Shiffer, Amy Silberkleit, Bryan Kress*

Dogan Point, HRM 39.5: From George's Island Park we watched two adult bald eagles perched, fifty feet apart, in a black oak on the south side of Dogan Point, less than a quarter-mile away. We had set spotting scopes up for a hundred birders who had joined us and we collectively agreed that this was a "pair" of eagles we were watching. We were wrong. A second adult joined one of them, landing only a few feet away. A short distance away, out over the Hudson, we could see a pair of adult bald eagles engaged in an aerial courtship display. *Andra Sramek, Dee Rod, Doug Rod, Kimberly Schwab, Christopher Letts, Tom Lake*

1/31 Poughkeepsie to Manhattan, HRM 75.5-5.5: I made sure to get a window seat on the 7:29 AM Metro North train from Poughkeepsie to Grand Central Station—over sixty miles of riverside travel. In Newburgh Bay, 15 miles downriver, the bow end of an empty oil barge was rising up over the thick ice, stalling the struggling tugboat behind it. The river was pretty solidly frozen for the first 24 miles south to West Point. Just south of Iona Island, a favorite bald eagle wintering site, three immature eagles were squabbling over something I could not make out from the speeding train. At the mouth of the Croton River there were two more immatures, one in plain view on the ice close by the tracks. I quickly glanced at the faces of passengers nearby; only one was looking out at the river, alert to the sight. "Young eagle," I said. "I wondered what it was," she replied. *Steve Stanne*

Croton River, HRM 34: A dozen birders from Greenbrook Sanctuary joined us to search for winter waterfowl on the Hudson. At the confluence of the Croton River with Croton Bay we spotted a male northern harrier, a "gray ghost," gliding over the grass of Croton Marsh. Female harriers are seen much more frequently. We counted three adult and seven immature bald eagles out on the ice, in the air, and in day perches along the bay. On the water we counted a dozen or more bufflehead ducks and a beautiful pair of hooded mergansers. *Bob Rancan, Janet Rancan, Nancy Slowik, Hallie Wolfe*

The term **"gray ghost"** is used by *Dick Miller,* senior hawk watcher for Greenbrook Sanctuary. It is an apt description of this sleek, light-colored raptor with black wingtips, that seems to float over the marsh and blend into the soft colors of winter. (See Dunne 1988:130.)

Red-tailed hawk   by Wayne Kocher

Verplanck, HRM 40.5: We had our spotting scopes set on a tall hardwood across the river on Stony Point. Three adult eagles were perched so close together that they all fit in the view of the forty power lens. An immature passed across in front of us and we were feeling pretty lucky. Someone called for us to turn around and look up. There, fifty feet over our heads peering down, was an adult bald eagle. There was silence among us, a reverent hush. For many in the group this was as close as they had ever been to an eagle in the wild. This eagle was not bothered by us but had just about enough of a single fish crow that was doing its best imitation of "mobbing." Spreading its huge wings, the eagle dropped down out of the tree, passed directly overhead, and crossed the river, with the crow in hot pursuit. Around the base of a light tower just south off Verplanck were a dozen hen and drake common mergansers. They were diving and coming up with small fish, probably white perch. A dozen ring-billed gulls were hovering a few feet overhead and trying to steal the fish from the mergansers as each surfaced after a dive. Several tug-of-wars ensured but the mergansers managed to keep their prizes. *Ron Stanford, Sandy Bonardi*

China Pier, HRM 43: When ice is on the river, there are few better places to view winter birds than from China Pier, just below Peekskill. On this day we had a group of birders with us. There was some open water in the channel, and along the edge of the ice we counted a dozen bald eagles (4 adults, eight immatures). Across nine miles and one hour, our birders counted twenty-seven bald eagles among thirty species of birds. *Tom Lake, Christopher Letts*

Croton Reservoir, HRM 34: A dozen bald eagles (4 adults, 3 immatures) were camped out on the ice, a quarter-mile east of the dam, near a small raft of American coot that were paddling around in an open lead. An adult eagle hovered over the coot and they dove. The eagle waited for them to resurface and, when they did, the eagle grabbed one, killed it on the ice, and began to pluck it. Within minutes an immature eagle stole the coot but it was immediately stolen back by another adult. With the coot secure in its talons, that eagle took off for the shoreline to perch and feed. *Robert Pearson Jr.*

Winter Thaw
There are icy patches everywhere,
Snow for you and me to share.
The wind is a nightmare,
But I do not really care.

Snow is falling on the ground,
Try not to make a sound.
For animals are walking around.

There might be an eagle in the sky,
Or maybe one right by your side.

Soon the ice will melt,
And the water will start to flow,
Then it will be time to go.
Christie Alvarez, New Windsor School, NY

February 2000

Bird and beast and tree and plant
are each vital points of contact with the vast whole,
and the self-same currents flow in each.
John Burroughs, *Field and Study*

2/1 New Hamburg to Croton-Harmon, HRM 67.5-34.5: I climbed aboard the 7:39 AM Metro North train and considered myself fortunate to find a window seat. This was the final morning "peak period" train to Manhattan's Grand Central Station. My stop would be Croton-Harmon, a 33-mile trip. From bank-to-bank, the river appeared frozen. As we raced past Brockway (HRM 63) I caught a quick glimpse of my first eagle, an adult, emerging from a dive on an open lead in the ice with something in its talons, a fish or duck, and then it was past and gone from sight. When we were abreast of Pollepel Island and the Bannerman castle (HRM 58) the severity of the ice became very apparent. In mid-river a Coast Guard vessel was hard at work clearing a path in the channel for a barge and tug that was stopped, surrounded by thick floes. On the south side of Constitution Island (HRM 52) a pair of adult bald eagles perched close together looking out over World's End. At Arden Point (HRM 50.5) an immature eagle eyed the train from a shoreline perch as we passed. Out on the ice off Highlands Falls (HRM 50) a pair of immatures rode an ice floe slowly downriver. At Con Hook (HRM 48.5), seven common goldeneye, mostly drakes flying in tight formation, breezed past the train heading downriver as though we were standing still. Off Iona Island a single immature eagle on an ice floe was breakfasting on a duck or a fish. It was standing on its meal making it impossible to determine which it was. Another immature was on the ice at Fish Island (HRM 44.5). As we passed the outlet from Annsville Creek (HRM 43.5), an open lead was filed with at least a hundred common mergansers. A few hundred feet away in Peekskill Bay an adult and two immature bald eagles kept watch. As we sped past China Pier I counted two more adults and two more immature eagles, though I may have missed seeing twice that number. Haverstraw Bay (HRM 38), in some places over three miles wide, tends to have broad stretches of fairly smooth ice. This morning much of the surface of the bay looked like a frosty pane of window glass lying on the water. There are few, if any, better ways to see the river in winter, than from a train ride along the Hudson. *Tom Lake*

World's End, between West Point Military Academy and Constitution Island, where the river makes a near 45° turn, is the deepest point in the Hudson at just over 200'.

Rime ice   by Esther Kiviat

Winter Bliss
Beauty beyond perception
Stands enveloped in white lace.
Nature reaches full perfection
In this enchanted place.

Frozen in time as it seems

River stationary in frost,
Tranquil now as it dreams
Of when serenity shall be lost.

Evidence of rushing currents
Lie imprinted upon the shore.
Spring may bring such wild torrents
As it has done in years before.

Mountains rise indifferently
With jutting peaks that cut the sky.
Glaring down haughtily
At those who dare to stand beside.

The sun is nearly blinding
When reflected by the snow.
Rocks and trees alike all shining
With a phosphorescent glow.

Only here can things so simple
Be quite so dazzling as this.
Only on the Hudson River
Could winter bring such bliss.
*Amanda Rogers, 8th Grade, Mahopac Middle
School, Mahopac, NY*

Croton Point, HRM 34: We were in four-wheel-drive, having traversed a snow field a foot-deep near Sarah's Point looking for winter waterfowl, when a large dark shape dropped down out of a red oak, wheeled fifty feet in front of us, and gave us a withering look. It was an immature bald eagle and in its talons was a fish. As it circled low overhead it paused momentarily in its flight, drew its legs forward up under its body closer to its head, to inspect the contents of its talons. It was still there—what appeared to us through our binoculars to be a half-eaten fish, perhaps a gizzard shad or striped bass. Content that it had not lost its lunch, the eagle landed in the top of another oak a few hundred feet away and continued its feed. We sat in the truck for 15 minutes and watched it tear and swallow, all the while keeping the meal securely pressed to the stout tree limb with its huge yellow feet. Each time it would bend to tear off another piece of fish, we could clearly see the broad white stripe from its nape down its back. This was

"Capeman," Croton Point's three-year-old white extreme. *Tom Lake, Christopher Letts*

Croton Point, HRM 35: It was like being in an old western movie. We were walking along the base of the 150' high landfill when we heard a thunderous roar from the other side coming our way. In the movie a thousand bison would have emerged from over the crest in a cloud of prairie dust and we would have yelled "stampede" and run for our lives. But in this case it was a thousand Canada geese, the most we had ever seen at one time on the Point. Wave after wave cleared the hill and swung to the east. We had our suspicions and, sure enough, there in the sky to the southwest were three bald eagles, two adults and one immature. The herd of geese had just about made its escape when the leading edge of the flock made a U-turn. It was geese bumping into geese, pandemonium and confusion, and a thousand birds now headed west. In their wake a fourth bald eagle, an immature, was making tiny circles in the sky. *Tom Lake, Christopher Letts*

Cardinal   by Wayne Kocher

Croton-on-Hudson, HRM 34.5: Our annual *Mahopac Middle School* train trip left the Croton-Harmon Train Station in late morning with 120 eighth-graders. We were all eager to see the Hudson River in winter and bald eagles on the ice. *Bob Miller, Betsy Walters*

Hudson Highlands, HRM 44-58: This was a very memorable experience seeing the Hudson River in winter from a train. Frozen completely over for the first time in about five years, the Hudson looked like a miniature mountain range. The mountains were covered with an untouched blanket of snow; the river was disguised in a series of geometric shapes—snow-covered ice. We felt very calm and peaceful as the icy, snow-covered river passed by our windows. The only voice we heard was from our guide; everyone was too fixated on the beauty to gossip. As we passed Fish Island, just above Dunderberg Mountain, we saw some gulls perched on the ice right next to a bald eagle. Every time we saw an eagle we got excited. Eagles have always been our favorite bird, probably because they are not as common as cardinals and bluebirds. As we passed World's End, the deepest spot on the Hudson, we saw three more eagles on Constitution Island. In a meadow on the island we saw a white-tailed deer, eyeing us as we passed. Storm King Mountain looked huge. Beneath it in the river we watched a Coast Guard ice breaker making a path for an oil barge and tugboat. The Hudson put on a dazzling show for us; it was a peaceful, serene feeling. It was like we were in our own little world, peering out our windows. Everyone deserves to experience the Hudson River in this way at least once in their life. *Kathryn Ferrara, Kimberly Cantone, Jennifer Naegeli, Jason Hernandez, Andrew Rose, Mahopac Middle School*

Poughkeepsie, HRM 75.5: As the Mahopac school busses rolled away we looked overhead to see an immature bald eagle soaring over the Poughkeepsie train station. When this day had ended, we figured that we had spotted as many as 33 different bald eagles (14 adults, 19 immatures) along the Hudson in the 41-mile reach between the Croton River in Westchester County and Poughkeepsie in Dutchess County. *Tom Lake, Christopher Letts*

2/2   West Point, HRM 52: Before we even scanned the early morning wintry riverscape, my colleague, *Chris Pray*, and I were compelled to observe an immense immature bald eagle in flight low over the jumble of ice floes. On sunny perches along the far shore of Constitution Island was a threesome of adults and, sitting apart, an immature. After a few minutes two ravens came cavorting across toward us, *"wonking"* and displaying their brand of aerial talent. Not so long ago this sighting might have been an apparition. Formerly rare even in migration, ravens now regularly grace this craggy part of the river. Their musical calls pervading the quiet ebb and flow, the North River is brought to life even on the coldest days. *Bob Kakerbeck*

North River is an older name, given by the Dutch, for the Hudson. The Delaware River was called the South River. The Algonkian-speaking Mahican Indians, four hundred years ago, called the Hudson River, *Mahicanituck*, roughly translated as, *"the river that flows both ways."* When the English took control of the valley in 1664, our river became known as the Hudson.

2/3   Kowawese, HRM 59: With steady snow flurries all morning, the park was like a winter wonderland. We set up spotting scopes for the students from *New Windsor Elementary* and the river provided us with a terrific show. The Hudson was snow-covered-ice, bank-to-bank, with only a thin dark ribbon in the channel where a tug and barge had plowed through. We spotted two immature bald eagles a short distance out on the ice, one of which had a large fish. Through the spotting scopes we could see that it was a gizzard shad. With as much cunning as it could muster, a red fox snuck out on the ice to try and steal the fish. The stealth of the fox could not match the eagle-eyes of the bird. The eagle waited until the last instant and then lifted off with the fish. Now we had a fox jumping up and down on the ice and an eagle hovering ten feet overhead teasing him. The eagle would fly a hundred feet, land, and begin to feed again. The fox would sneak over and prepare to pounce; the eagle would lift off; the fox would leap at empty air. This scenario was repeated three times. It reminded us of Lucy holding the football for Charlie Brown. We were captivated. After 15 unsuccessful minutes of trying to get the fish, the fox ambled off over

85

the ice toward Cornwall. For almost two hours we had three immature bald eagles flying back and forth in front of us giving everyone a close look. They were so close that our spotting scopes and binoculars were unnecessary. Near the end of the program, a teacher with some students down on the beach yelled for us to "Look!" The students and I looked just offshore and saw a pair of adult bald eagles in a courtship display. They were grabbing talons, flipping on their backs in the air, touching wings, doing short free-falls, and, as my colleague, *Chris Letts,* likes to say, "renewing their marriage vows" (most bald eagles mate for life). If five eagles and a red fox were not enough, out near the channel an adult harbor seal was hauled out on an ice floe for all to see. We had a spotting scope on it for a half hour and all of the students lined up to take a peek. *Barbara Oliver, Donna Sutton, Tom Lake, Christopher Letts*

The Eagle's Day
The Eagle wakes up to find some food,
It flies over the ice and looks for prey.
The Eagle sees a fish,
And flies down to scoop it up.
The fish is very big,
And the Eagle cannot fly away.
As the Eagle stands on the ice,
A fox see the fish and tries to sneak up,
But the Eagle sees the fox.
The fox tries and tries to get the fish,
But it has no luck.
The fox leaves and the Eagle goes home.
Antonio Diaz, New Windsor Elementary School, NY

2/5   George's Island, HRM 39: High school students from Crown Heights and Bedford-Stuyvesant, in Brooklyn, were out for a day on the river courtesy of Friends of Fishes, Inc. It was cold (18°F) and the north wind made it feel like zero. We set up two spotting scopes along the shoreline and doled out binoculars for viewing. Before long we were literally surrounded by bald eagles: they were in the air, on the ice, and perched close by in trees. It was like being at a three-ring circus and not knowing where to look first! It was not difficult finding

someone who had never seen an eagle before, because none of them had. Bed-Sty students *Johnathan Figueroa, Ken Vinson, Kimberly Vinson,* and *Quiana Young,* exclaimed that, for them, it was a spiritual moment. We saw 23 eagles in total (8 adults, 15 immatures). *Yelena Olevskaia, Sofiya Masterovoy, Maciej Samela, Anton Masterovoy, David Rokoszynski, Clive Richards, Ricardo Sealy, Tom Lake, Christopher Letts*

Eagle watcher at George's Island   by Tom Lake

2/6   George's Island, HRM 39: On some days, getting to the park at 10:30 AM would mean missing the "eagle show." But this morning I was greeted by 4 adults and 6 immatures. Two immatures and one adult were circling over the river just offshore making a continuous air-to-water-to-air cycle with a large fish. One of the birds would drop the fish (a big splash!). Another would dive, pick it off the water, rise, and then drop it again. The three of them went through this routine for several minutes, each in turn. Was this play? It looked like a training exercise. *Gene Heinemeyer*

2/7   Blue Point, HRM 73.5: The crew working local freight WPKI80 aboard CSX locomotive 2807, engineer *Earl Pardini*, conductor *Ted Allen*, and brakeman *Dick Grace*, spotted two adult bald eagles out on the river off Blue Point. The larger of the pair, probably a female, was flying east to west about six feet over the ice toward a small cove inside the railroad tracks. When it was within a few hundred feet of us, it was startled by the train. It turned back to the river, was joined by the second adult, and together they flew south.

2/8   Verplanck, 40.5: We watched four bald eagles that were directly across the river from Steamboat Dock. They were perched in two trees just below the Stony Point Lighthouse. Two more joined them to make six. One pair took off and we watched them soar and swirl together for about 15 minutes before they headed north. What a spectacular sight! We could watch them forever. *Diane Picciano, Philip Picciano*

Croton Point, HRM 34: Two immature bald eagles were circling and touching wings over the landfill. They called repeatedly in a loud, shrill squeal. Another immature bird stood on the ice on the south shore. Six eagles, a mix of adults and immatures, perched in the hardwoods along the south side of the Point. Another immature perched in a snag by the path around the base of the landfill and yet another immature perched in a cottonwood by the Croton River railroad. Eleven bald eagles in view. From the top of the landfill we could see an immature eagle dive with legs extended and pluck a large fish out of Croton Bay. It flew to shore where three more eagles materialized to "share" the meal, closely followed by three crows. The possessor of the fish raised its wings in a threat and the others backed off for a moment before moving in again. Wings raised, the eagles hopped up and down on the sand. The fish, probably a gizzard shad, was dropped and retrieved several times by different birds before

one immature picked it up in its talons and flapped heavily to another stretch of beach, with crows in hot pursuit. *Amy Silberkleit, Michael Shiffer, Isis Shiffer, Elijah Shiffer*

2/9   Annsville Bay, HRM 43.5: This mild morning had cardinals and titmice singing their spring songs. Canada geese vociferously announced their interest in the real estate market and their intent to defend and hold the best "location, location, location!" In shoreline thickets a small flock of bluebirds did their best to out-blue the sky. *Christopher Letts*

Dogan Point, HRM 39.5: On late afternoons in winter, bald eagles seem to congregate on the south side of Dogan Point to avoid the wind and soak in the last warm rays of sunlight. This afternoon they were there a bit early. At 3:00 PM, I counted six adult eagles perched in the oaks and pines. *Ed Stinson*

2/11   Croton Marsh, HRM 34: Some birders prefer blue-sky days, other relish the adversity of the elements. *Eric Bender* and his sixty sixth graders from *MS113 School* in the Bronx had no choice. We had driving rain and heavy fog, thick as Boston chowder. Under these circumstances, we were thrilled to see the silhouettes of a pair of bald eagles in a cottonwood tree overlooking Croton Marsh. Our spotting scopes brought the birds right into the students faces. Out of the gloom, one of the eagles turned and glared at us. One young man, looking in the scope at that moment, recoiled as though that eagle had reached out and grabbed his tongue. He sputtered and stammered but managed to say, "Cool." A while later, a short distance upriver at Verplanck, we spotted a great cormorant out on an ice floe. *Christopher Letts, Andra Sramek, Tom Lake*

2/12   Croton Point to Bear Mountain, HRM 34-46: A field trip of the *Linneaen Society* in search of bald eagles along the Hudson River proved to be very productive. From Croton Point to Bear Mountain an astounding 56 bald eagles were counted (8 adults, 48 immatures). Twenty birds were in Croton Bay, 24 more were found from George's Island to Bear Mountain, and nine were seen at the Croton Dam (Croton Reservoir). Counting single birds we viewed in transit, the total count was 67 eagles. Other sightings included two ravens and forty common redpolls. *John Askildsen*

2/13   Farmer's Landing, HRM 67: Mixed messages of winter and spring: At dawn it was 9°F and yet the male cardinals were singing their April song. *Tom Lake*

George's Island, HRM 39: *John Moyle* of Scarsdale Audubon found a great horned owl pellet containing the remains of a long-eared owl.

Because **owls** swallow their prey whole, a squirrel, a duckling, or the neighbor's cat, the non-nutritive parts must be expelled. That includes bones, feathers, fur, teeth, tone-nails, and the exoskeleton of insects and other invertebrates, everything that will not digest. Once the usable portion of what they have eaten is digested, the owl's stomach muscles contract to compress the unused parts into a compact pill-shaped mass. This pellet is then regurgitated or "coughed up" by the owl. Pellets can be dissected to unveil the bones of the prey item, which in turn can be used to reconstruct their skeleton (the skulls of mammals can be used to identify the species). Regurgitated pellets are also common in gulls and raptors. *Rich Anderson*

Oscawana Island, HRM 38.5: Offshore in Haverstraw Bay we spotted a half-dozen adult and immature bald eagles on ice floes amidst scores of common mergansers and bufflehead ducks. Two immature eagles were in full play for our scopes. They alternately carried a large fish, dropped it in the water with a big splash, retrieved it, and the chase was on again. These brought our four-mile China Pier-to-George's Island total to 20 bald eagles (9 adults and 11 immatures). *Ellen Hake, Tom Hake, Brad Hake, Henrietta Hake, Ben Yazgi, Christopher Letts, Tom Lake*

Croton Point, HRM 34: The lower road that runs along Croton Marsh has always been favored by owls. The thick and sheltered stands

of white pine make perfect habitat. On the way back from Sarah's Point today, I saw two long-eared owls. Then along the lower road, flying out of a white pine, was a barred owl. *John Moyle*

2/17   Hunter's Brook, HRM 67.5: It was a couple of hours into the ebb tide and, combined with snow melt, the water was rushing out of Hunter's Brook, a small Wappinger Creek tributary about a mile inland from the Hudson. In a clear, open lead I could see a half dozen 2-3 pound gizzard shad facing upstream in the current, gently swaying back and forth, looking for food to be swept downstream. They were plainly visible, and vulnerable, in two feet of water. They would have been an easy catch for a hungry eagle. *Tom Lake*

2/19   Farmer's Landing, HRM 67: It was the morning after seven inches of new snow had fallen. The river ice was capped with white. Across the way over Cedarcliff a flock of gulls was in the air, agitated, flying in circles. Something had spooked them. Looking just beyond them I could see the large, flat-winged form of an immature bald eagle rising from its night roost, heading for a day perch. *Christopher Lake*

Croton Bay, HRM 34: There were eleven bald eagles here this morning. Observations indicate that gizzard shad is the food fish of choice for these wintering eagles. Up to several pounds in weight, present in shoal waters in large numbers, it is the right size and in the right place for the birds. With the late-winter striped bass fishing drawing up to twenty boats a day to Croton Bay, stories are being told of fishermen accidently hooking up to a dozen gizzard shad a day. In the Croton estuary they are striking small jigs and shad darts cast by local youngsters to the thick schools as they pass by. *Christopher Letts*

2/20   Farmer's Landing, HRM 67: In late afternoon I stopped my car along the river hoping to see an eagle. I was told that this was the spot. I looked up and right overhead was an adult bald eagle soaring in great circles against a bright blue sky. This was only the second time I had ever seen a bald eagle, and the first in the Hudson Valley. *Mary Brockway*

Croton Point, HRM 34.5: The Saw Mill River Audubon Society spotted two long-eared owls in a stand of white pines near the RV parking area at Croton Point Park.

Sandy Hook Bay, NJ: It was a beautiful wintry day for about twenty birders on our Winter Waterfowl Hike. Our sightings ranged from a flock of snow buntings to a northern harrier to three harbor seals basking on a sand bar in Sandy Hook Bay. A Bonaparte's gull swooped among other gulls and on the water we spotted greater scaup, American coot, canvasbacks, Canada geese, mute swans, and double-crested cormorants. Along the shore we saw a great blue heron. Our first red-winged blackbirds of the season were here. *Dery Bennett, Lynn Hunt, Pam Carlsen*

2/21 Cedarcliff, HRM 67: The crew of CSX KI80 reported two adult bald eagles perched on the side of Cedarcliff, an immature soaring overhead, and a heart-shaped balloon caught in a tree. *Earl Pardini, Ted Allen, Dick Grace, Wayne Deyo, trainmaster, Kingston.*

Hudson Valley: A new "eagle nest" was being constructed. A pair of adult bald eagles were breaking off small limbs with their beaks, transferring the branches to their talons in midair, carrying them to the site, and then placing the limbs in the crotch of a tree. *Chip Putman*

Eagle nests are hard to miss when you happen upon one. Given the size and activity of eaglets, fledglings, and their parents, you can assume that their nests are large. Eagle nests grow in size each season as more material is added. The "record nest," from Florida, was reported to be 22' deep and more than 2,000 pounds when it finally brought down the tree it was in. More typical New York State nests are up to ten-feet deep and seven-feet across. Ornithologist *Heinz Meng* once described an eagle's nest as "looking like a Volkswagen stuck up in a tree." The exact locations of active Hudson Valley bald eagle nests are protected for the safety and security of the birds.

Croton River to China Pier, HRM 34-43: I had been seeing from one to two dozen eagles on a daily basis and was curious about the effect of the latest siege of snow, ice, and cold weather. Apparently it shook things up in the eagle world. At the Croton River I saw three eagles, three more at Oscawana Island, five rode the ice at George's Island, and the same number were perched at Stony Point across the river from Steamboat Dock in Verplanck. In Peekskill I walked to the end of China Pier and set up a spotting scope—and gasped. Out on the pack ice were forty—count 'em, forty—eagles catching a ride on the down tide. The wind was calm, the sun was warm, and they all seemed to be content to let the current move them. Four of the young birds had their backs to the sun, wings fully extended in the manner of cormorants, drying off. I wondered if they were drying off from a dive or just soaking up the warmth of the sun. Fifty-six bald eagles! *Christopher Letts*

2/22 Verplanck, HRM 40.5: It was a clear, blue-sky mid-afternoon at Steamboat Dock. There were ice floes out in the river between Verplanck and the Stony Point lighthouse. We spotted an adult bald eagle flying across the Hudson from Stony Point to Steamboat Dock, then directly over our heads—no binoculars needed. Four juveniles were out on the ice fighting over a fish. One took off with the fish but dropped it after being pursued. It was then picked up by another immature. This wild "fish ball" game went on for about five minutes. The victor then retreated to the trees at Stony Point. (We are obsessed with these birds and need to see them at least twice a day!) *Diane Picciano*

Edgewater, NJ, HRM 8.5: It was barely a half hour to low tide on the Hudson between Edgewater and Fort Lee. Along the shoreline I could see oysters by the hundreds clinging to the exposed rocks. At first I thought they were just shells but I went down for a closer look: live oysters! They ranged in size (valve height) from 24-69 mm. *Glenn Blank*

Roseton, HRM 65.2: The crew of CSX locomotive KI80 spotted an adult bald eagle out on the ice just south of Danskammer Point. Two more adults were sitting on the ice a little further south off the Hess tank farm near the mouth of Middlehope Brook. *Earl Pardini, Ted Allen, Dick Grace, and Wayne Deyo, trainmaster, Kingston.*

Cold Spring, HRM 54: On the front lawn of the Boscobel grounds I spotted an adult and an immature bald eagle. The adult had a yellow tag on its upper right wing. They took off, soared overhead, and then dropped down into Foundry Cove marsh. They made my day! *Andra Sramek*

Croton Point, HRM 34.5: A short-eared owl was gliding over the landfill, hunting for rodents in the dusk. The owl dropped to the ground and disappeared in the weeds, blending in with the dry stalks. Then it rose again on long wings and glided slowly, turning its head around to scan the ground. Three hundred male red-winged blackbirds gathered in the branches of a tree near the marsh. They were jockeying for perches on the uppermost branches and calling harshly. *Amy Silberkleit, Michael Shiffer, Isis Shiffer, Elijah Shiffer*

2/24   Mill Pond, HRM 90: It was early morning when I spotted three swans in the open water of Mill Pond along the river a couple of miles north of Vanderburgh Cove. As they climbed out of the water and up on the ice I noticed that two of them, with black bills, were tundra swans. The third was a mute swan. *Susan Joseph*

Tundra swans are often called "America's native swan." Their common name refers to their summer nesting range north of Hudson Bay in the arctic tundra. They can usually be heard calling long before they are seen, which leads to another frequently used colloquial name, trumpeter swan. Tundra swans are occasional visitors to the Hudson Valley during spring and fall migration.

Fishkill Creek, HRM 60: The tidal Fishkill Creek at Madam Brett Park was busy with feeding waterfowl. We saw 4 beautiful male wood ducks, 5 common mergansers, 5 ring-necked ducks, 5 green-winged teals, a pair of buffleheads, 2 black ducks, and several mallards. We heard nine hooded mergansers making funny noises that we had not heard before—the males were courting the females. As we were turning to leave, we spotted a brown creeper working a nearby tree. As an end to a wonderful morning, an adult bald eagle flew up the creek. *Allan Michelin, Barbara Michelin*

Cornwall Bay, HRM 59: At dusk I watched a pair of red foxes walk slowly across the ice of Cornwall Bay. A little earlier there had been seven immature bald eagles out on the bay, one of which appeared to have a duck or a fish, and two adults perched in the sycamores along the shore. *Chip Putnam*

2/25   Roa Hook, HRM 44: I sat over a foot of ice, hauling up yellow perch and bluegill sunfish, and wishing for just one more month of winter. While I caught my dinner, spring arrived nonetheless. Flocks of red-winged blackbirds and grackles appeared. Carolina wrens, cardinals, titmice and mourning doves poured out their songs, and killdeer pecked for grit on the beach. Hat and gloves in my pocket, I slipped off the ice and tiptoed through a cloud of blooming snowdrops on my way to the truck. *Christopher Letts*

2/26   Norrie Point, HRM 85: Eleven eagles and 314 people showed up for our annual NYSDEC Hudson River Estuary Program Bald Eagle Watch. At 8:00 AM an adult eagle was perched only 200' away along the shore. It soon joined its mate in the top of a pine tree in mid-river on Esopus Island and then gave us four hours of viewing enjoyment. Another adult pair from upriver joined in. A couple hundred yards north an immature eagle perched in a hardwood overlooking an open lead from the Indian Kill. The open water was filled with common mergansers, all within the shadow of the eagle, yet none of them seem disturbed. An hour later an adult eagle had replaced the immature, and the open water below the perch was empty. With the switch in birds, the mergansers had left. Hungry eyes may have replaced sated ones. As many as seven immatures eagles—one a "white extreme"—perched along the edge of the ice near the free-running channel. Behind them, several dozen common mergansers were swimming, nearly within talon reach. The eagles appeared to be picking food out of the ice. *Alex Papo* and his mom, *Laura*, saw their first eagles in the wild, as did six-year-old *Rosemary Compton*. With our spotting scopes bringing the birds, as many as five at a time, seemingly to within arms' reach, the reaction from the spectators was a sustained, "Wow!" *Karl Beard, Nancy Beard, Annika Beard, Christopher Beard, Jean Drusik, Michael Hargraves, Barbara Hargraves, Tom Lake*

Eagle watch at Norrie Point   by Tom Lake

Eagles and eagle food are a poorly understood relationship. An explosion of gulls or waterfowl into the air often means a hungry eagle is soaring nearby. The sky over cornfields in Saratoga County will fill with hundreds of snow geese from the presence of a single eagle on the wing. But just as often ducks will swim, seemingly without a care, within a wingbeat of a perched eagle. Crows will share scraps from a fish dinner while standing within talon reach. It suggests that other birds might be able to sense when an eagle is hungry and when they might be in danger. Is there a gleam in the eye of an eagle?

Sprout Brook, HRM 43.5: I had been watching bald eagle courtship behavior with great delight—those aerial ballets we refer to as "sky dancing." The 15 eagles at Peekskill's historic China Pier had been active and my thoughts were still on their breathtaking aerobatics as I headed for home. I made a stop to check a small flock of waterfowl at Sprout Book swimming pool and spotted two big, dark birds emulating the flight I had just observed at China Pier—swooping, swirling flight, tightly synchronized. The courting black vultures had me fooled for a few seconds. Then back to the ducks. What could they be doing in this shallow, mostly ice-covered pool, devoid of life as far as I knew? The binoculars revealed a pair of mallards, a black duck, a female goldeneye, a male ring-necked duck, and three pairs of hooded mergansers. A troupe of newly-arrived killdeer lined the edge of the pool. *Christopher Letts*

2/29 Hudson Highlands: With the increased number of wintering eagles in this reach of the valley due to heavy icing upriver, it seemed logical that an increased number of night roosts would be required to accommodate them. A careful search of likely places disclosed some locations of which we were previously unaware. At one in particular we watched, from an appropriate distance, no fewer than 35 eagles perched in hardwoods, silhouetted against the sky in the fading light of dusk. *Lou Kingsley, Jesse Jaycox, Pete Nye, Craig Thompson, Eric Lind*

Baird Park, HRM 75.5: I've been watching this great blue heron rookery in the Fishkill Creek watershed for 15 years. The first few great blues were already on their nests, a full week earlier than in other years. They are such a magnificent bird. *Brian Connolly*

Spring

March 2000

Nothing ever really goes to waste in an estuary.
When a plant or animal dies, bacteria, shrimps, crabs, eels,
and other scavengers feed upon it and help recycle the nutrients.
The rocking action of the tides keeps the lower Hudson stirred like a thick soup.
Robert H. Boyle, *The Hudson, A Natural and Unnatural History*

3/1   Highland to Plum Point (Kowawese), HRM 75-59: The weather was spring-like with a chilly breeze as the CSX locomotive 2807 made its way south along the river. We spotted an adult eagle out on the ice just above the Mid-Hudson Bridge, another on the ice in front of Danskammer Point, and a third adult perched on the hillside at Plum Point. *Earl Pardini, Ted Allen, Dickie Grace*

The River is
Silent and frozen,
Peaceful and nonthreatening,
Cold and icy.
Exciting.
Brian Moriarity, New Windsor School, NY

Croton Point, HRM 34: At this time of the year, when there is a great uproar from flocks of gulls and waterfowl, it is a very good bet that an eagle is approaching. Most of the time prey items turn out to be fish, but now and again there is evidence that the panicked flights are warranted. A drift of belly feathers and goosedown marked the spot where an eagle had taken down, plucked, and eaten a Canada goose. Geese are not convenient to carry and are eaten where they are killed. *Christopher Letts*

3/2   Farmer's Landing, HRM 67: Con Rail locomotive 8657 moved steadily north along the western shoreline under Soap Hill. An adult bald eagle was perched on a limb not more than a dozen feet over the train as it moved past.

Trains are a common occurrence for wintering eagles and are apparently not feared. A westerly wind had pushed much of the river ice over to the east side leaving the channel and the western side open. At two hours from the top of the flood tide, the loose floe ice was moving upriver in the current. An immature bald eagle had sat down on a tiny chunk in mid-channel that appeared no larger than a frisbee. *Tom Lake*

Horned grebe   by Wayne Kocher

Wappinger Creek, HRM 67.5: At the mouth of the creek, perched on the horizontal limb of a sycamore, was a "dirty bird." A sub-adult bald eagle, in its fourth year, shares plumage with both adults and immatures and has a dirty-white look to its head and tail. This bird stayed in the sycamore for over an over, trying out several different limbs, all the while keeping a sharp eye out for opportunities in the now ice-free tidal Wappinger. *Tom Lake*

China Pier, HRM 43: Out on the ice, not more than a hundred yards from the parking lot, a juvenile bald eagle was feasting on a bufflehead duck. The eagle was ringed by fish crows that seemed to me to be taking some serious chances, but the eagle was entirely engrossed by its meal. I'm always impressed at the slow, careful way they feed—the word "fastidious" comes to mind. A second eagle landed close beside the first, this one a third-year white extreme, maybe the one we have come to call "Capeman." Both birds seemed amicably disposed, and the first one continued feeding. Four more juvenile birds appeared over the parking lot and began an air show that went on for twenty minutes. Swoops, dives, 360° rolls, talon grapples, flying upside down—the things they can do in the air! The two eagles on the ice soon joined the airborne birds, and the show went on. The fish crows were dispossessed by a pair of black-backed gulls, all that patient waiting for nothing. *Christopher Letts*

3/3   Stillwell Lake, HRM 46.5: The West Point Military Academy daily eagle survey crew spotted an immature golden eagle on Stillwell Lake just above Popolopen Creek. This is a once in every five or six-years phenomenon. The last one I saw in winter at West Point was 1992. They also saw an adult and an immature bald eagle. *Jim Beemer*

3/4   Minerva, HRM 58: Although it was chilly and we had two-feet of snow on the ground, the first migrants of spring, a cloud of red-winged blackbirds and a lesser number of common grackles, descended from the sky to the red oaks, sugar maples, white pines, and then to the single feeder in our yard. Pushing aside the chickadees, they rudely assaulted the sunflower seeds before moving on. *Mike Corey,* Sue Corey

Trail to the High Peaks   by Tom Lake

Denning Point, HRM 60: We were hiking into the Fishkill Creek inlet at Denning Point Cove when we saw two immature bald eagles and one that appeared to be in transition, eclipse plumage, a four-year-old about to get its adult feathers. *Steve Seymour, Lisa Seymour*

Garrison, HRM 52: We saw a peregrine falcon at Constitution Marsh. Mourning cloak butterflies and killdeer are around. The fuse is lit for the springtime explosion. *Eric Lind*

Sugarloaf Hill, HRM 49.5: On our way to the top of Sugarloaf, through a large grove of dead hemlocks, we heard the loud *"Wuk"* call of a pileated woodpecker. Two adults were pecking and hammering on the trees and calling as they flew from trunk to trunk. Bounding up the barkless trunks, they were red and black, and huge, like prehistoric birds. At the edge of a pond we saw a green frog and a tadpole before they darted back under the thin film of ice which remained on the surface. From the top of Sugarloaf we could see Manitou Marsh, Anthony's Nose and the Bear Mountain Bridge to the south. *Amy Silberkleit, Michael Shiffer, Isis Shiffer, Elijah Shiffer*

3/5   Fort Miller, HRM 192.5: I was surprised to see such a broad stretch of geese both downriver and up beyond the Lock 6 dam, extending a mile north to the tail waters of Thompson Island. I estimated at least a thousand Canada geese and, among them, 15-20 snow geese. Ducks, goldeneye, ring-neck, scaup, and common mergansers, were also sprinkled among the geese beneath cumulus clouds and a robin's-egg-blue sky. The river was completely free of ice, running strongly shore to shore, and the air resonated with unrelenting goose gabble. *Jim Sotis*

3/7   Haverstraw, HRM 36: Members of the Elks Club reported watching a harbor seal haul out on a pier. As the crowd gathered for a better look the seal slipped back into the river and disappeared. *Christopher Letts*

Croton Point, HRM 35: On this balmy late-winter day we saw an immature northern shrike perched like a sentinel on a pole, searching the just-mowed landfill cap for exposed voles. Its black eye patches and raptor-like beak gave it a fierce aspect. The bird dropped off the pole, flew just above the stubble, then rose to land on another pole. We heard the ringing, *"Cheery, cheery, cherry,"* song of a Carolina wren coming from an oak grove. *Amy Silberkleit, Michael Shiffer, Isis Shiffer, Elijah Shiffer*

Northern Shrike is a boreal songbird species whose presence in the Hudson Valley in winter is often associated with severe weather to the north. They have a raptor-like appearance and will often impale their prey, smaller song birds, on thorns and barbed wire. This has earned them the scientific name *Lanius excubitor*, which means "butcher."

Croton Reservoir, HRM 34: Yesterday, as I walked out across the Croton Dam looking for eagles, I saw a raft of forty common mergansers busy fishing. A quarter mile away, a drake merganser was swimming around and around an object in the water. I wondered about it—that continued for 15 minutes, all the time I was there. Today the same scenario. A raft of mergansers fishing and all the way across the dam face a drake merganser circling, circling, but now much closer and I could see that it was a dead hen merganser floating with neck outstretched. The drake never moved more than two feet away, and sometimes seemed to be touching the female with its bill. We think of geese and eagles as mating for life, but I never thought of other forms of waterfowl in that regard. *Christopher Letts*

3/8   Wappinger Creek, HRM 67.5: It was the dawn of a day when warm southerly breezes would produce a record-tying air temperature of 68°F—quite un-March-like. The sub-adult bald eagle was again perched at the mouth of the creek on the horizontal limb of a sycamore peering down at the emerging tide flats. It was near low tide and perhaps the warming pools left by the ebb tide contained fish. This eagle's behavior reminded me of a kingfisher, though I doubt the eagle would dive for a three-inch killifish. *Tom Lake*

3/10   Hudson Valley: This was our third warm winter in a row. December 1999 through February 2000 was the warmest recorded in the 105 years of record-keeping by the U.S. Government. It surpassed winter 1998-1999, which was the second warmest, surpassing winter 1997-1998, that had been the third warmest. *National Climate Data Center*

West Shokan, HRM 92: After several days of listening for bullfrogs, without result, we heard them for the first time this morning—in full chorus—in a small pond alongside Route 28A. *Jane Bierhorst, Jack Bierhorst*

Croton Bay, HRM 34: The unseasonably warm March weather produced a week of outrageous striped bass fishing in Croton Bay for *Gino Garner* and *Midgie Taube*. "We killed 'em!" was their recollection, figuratively speaking, of course. It was catch and release all you wanted on bass from 8-12 pounds, on everything from bottom-hugging leadhead jigs to swimming plugs. *Christopher Letts*

3/11 New Hamburg, HRM 67.5: *John Scardefield* died today. If you were not a riverman or a shad fisherman you might never have known. He fished in relative anonymity each spring for forty years, drifting his two miles from Clinton Point south to Diamond Reef—the fickle currents at the end of that run often resulted in his net getting hung down on the Reef. *Henry Gourdine*, a master commercial fisherman in Ossining for 75 years, when asked what it takes to be a good commercial fisherman would reply, with a twinkle in his eye, "Strong arms, a strong back, and a weak mind." John Scardefield was the exception; while strong as a ox, he also had a brilliant mind. He was a superb craftsman, building his own boats, nets, and cuddys. For forty years, the quality of John's fishing operation had no peers. John's love for the river and its fish began sixty years ago. He was a "buoy boy" for *Eddie Shea*, a legendary Hudson River shad fisherman himself. One day Eddie Shea caught a huge shad, the largest anyone had ever seen. When it came ashore John got a branch, laid it alongside the fish, and broke off the end. That stick measured 29¼"—a monster shad! John kept that stick for the rest of his life. Every spring we would hear the story of the stick, and John would go out and try to catch its equal. John was *Ahab* in search of his "Moby Dick." Now we have inherited John's stick, and we will keep up his search. *Steven Scardefield, Tom Lake*

Buoy boys once had an important job aboard Hudson River commercial fishing boats, particularly those who used drift nets for American shad. Children in riverside communities who were too young to throw or pull nets, but old enough to be useful, were hired by shad fishermen like *Eddie Shea* and *DeWit Robinson* (former captain of the *Alexander Hamilton* sidewheeler). For a quarter a drift, the buoy boys would wind the twine and stack the wooden buoys

attached to the top seamline of the nets as they came into the boat. The fisherman would pick the net (take out the shad) and the buoy boy would make sure the net stacked properly in the cuddy. Buoy boys were not only sharing in the excitement of the moment, but were being trained to be the commercial fishermen of the future. Today, with the advent of monofilament nets, poly-core float lines, and the distractions of daily life, buoy boys have become extinct.

Diamond Reef, HRM 67.5: One winter day many years ago, *John Scardefield* was ice fishing in mid-river off New Hamburg over Diamond Reef. At noon he left his gear in place, trudged over the ice to shore, walked a block to his house, and had lunch. A little over an hour later he walked back to the shore and looked out at Diamond Reef, a quarter-mile away. He saw nothing but open water. The tide had turned and the current had taken the ice, and his gear, away. *Tom Lake*

Albany High School student sampling Patroon Creek
by Doug Reed

Postscript:
New Hamburg, HRM 67.5: During the spring commercial fishing season, at the end of a drift, we scattered John's ashes on Diamond Reef. We let our shad net get hung down on the Reef in John's honor. *Steven Scardefield, Gale Collins, Stacy Scardefield*

3/12 Farmer's Landing, HRM 67: Across the river over Cedarcliff a lone immature bald eagle soared. As I caught it in my binoculars I could see in the background, far away to the west, a ragged skein of geese heading north. Given their flight formation and the fact that they were much too high to hear their call, I had to guess either brant or snow geese. Brant generally pass through in late April or early May. This was the right time for snow geese. *Tom Lake*

Verplanck, HRM 40.5: *Jimmy Carey* died yesterday, the same day as *John Scardefield.* These two commercial fishermen fished two different rivers, or so it seemed, Jimmy Carey the brackish lower river primarily with fixed gear, and John Scardefield the freshwater upriver primarily with drift nets. But they had much in common as well. They were both goodwill ambassadors for the river at a time when communities focused on the Hudson as an economic provider. Jimmy fished for fifty years, for blue crabs, striped bass, American shad, and his favorite, Atlantic sturgeon. Jimmy and his partners made some of the best sturgeon caviar on the river, much of which was sold at Fulton Market in Manhattan. Jimmy Carey, as much as any riverman I have ever known, was always eager to share a good story, talk about the river, or teach someone his trade. He was the consummate gentleman. Jimmy's smile, grace, and love of the river will be sorely missed. *Tom Lake*

3/15   Beacon, HRM 61: In a small pond a mile or so back from the river, I spotted an Iceland gull mixed in with some ring-billed gulls and a few mallards. *Rich Anderson*

The **Iceland gull**, which *Roger Tory Peterson* called a "pale ghostly gull," is rare in the Hudson Valley. These are arctic breeders that winter along the North Atlantic coast. Most Hudson Valley sightings are strays during migration or are the result of being blown here by nor'easters.

3/16   Soap Hill, HRM 67: At dawn I could see five adult bald eagles perched in a small area, tucked back in the trees halfway up Soap Hill. With the mild nights, this may have been a temporary night roost. Two of them, perhaps a mated pair, we perched so close they touched. The other three adults were scattered about on

other limbs but the entire area had a radius of no more than fifty feet. *Tom Lake*

Sandy Hook, NJ: This morning we witnessed the arrival of our first osprey of the season to the Visitor's Center nesting platform. This was the earliest date, since 1988, that I had recorded their return. *Pam Carlsen, Dery Bennett*

Springtime Osprey Return to Sandy Hook, NJ

1988	3/25	1995	3/22
1989	3/21	1996	3/28
1990	3/21	1997	3/27
1991	3/19	1998	3/25
1992	3/25	1999	3/24
1993	3/30	2000	3/16
1994	3/29		

3/17   Soap Hill, HRM 67: At first light, through several inches of new snow, I could spot only one adult bald eagle perched in a hardwood across the river on Soap Hill. Determining when eagles leave each March for their breeding grounds in Canada is a very inexact science. For the past week I had seen only half of the Cedarcliff pair at one time. Either they are being elusive or one of them has left. *Tom Lake*

Bald eagle adult pairs usually arrive and depart wintering locations separately. Whether heading to a familiar nest at the breeding grounds or a favorite feeding perch in the wintering territory, their travel is ordinarily a singular trip, but the destination is mutual. *Pete Nye*

For more information on the migration of Hudson Valley wintering Bald Eagles, visit on the Internet:
http://www.learner.org/jnorth

3/19   Flowed Land, HRM 311: We skied and walked up the 3.7 mile snow-covered Calamity Brook trail in the High Peaks to Flowed Land. It was sunny and 30°F. We saw many blowdowns and landslides from last fall's hurricane-turned-tropical storm *Floyd,* including a large grove of white cedar along the road from Henderson Lake. There were black-capped chickadees, ravens, and hoards of springtails (minute 6 mm insects) all over the snow along Calamity Brook. A post-dinner chill along the shore of Flowed Land sent us downstream in the twilight under the rising full moon. *Doug Reed, Peg Winship, Melissa Everrett, Will Nixon*

Lock 2, HRM 168: We pulled off to the side of Route 4 to get a look at some waterfowl that had caught our eye out on the river. Through binoculars we counted no fewer than thirty wood ducks (we missed a few more) along with a pair of hooded mergansers. *Tom Lake, Christopher Letts*

Saratoga National Historic Park, HRM 178: As we drove north along Route 4 we spotted a large, dark raptor heading straight at us, about a hundred feet over the highway. We pulled over and looked out our windows. Directly above, glancing down as it passed, was an immature bald eagle. A mile up the road we spotted rafting waterfowl; the narrow river was choked with ducks and geese. We estimated that in a quarter-mile of river there were a thousand Canada geese, 300 snow geese, and 400 mixed ducks including some pintails. *Tom Lake, Christopher Letts*

Thompson Island Pool, HRM 192.5: The irony of this surreal scene never fails to impress. We watched a thousand waterfowl share a short stretch of river, as a stopover on spring migration, separated from reputedly-toxic PCBs by the depth of the water and a layer of silt. The pool had many discreet rafts of ducks and geese. We guessed that there were 500 Canada geese and 250 snow geese, along with smaller numbers of ring-necked ducks and greater scaup. We also spotted several pied-billed grebes and one horned grebe. *Tom Lake, Christopher Letts*

Vernal Equinox

3/20 Ice Meadows, HRM 245: It was the dawn of spring but winter still held the upper Hudson in its grip. The river flowed through walls of ice, 15'-20' high. A half-dozen common mergansers drifted in the current with a single male common goldeneye hanging out on the edge of the group.

Boreas River, HRM 284: The full 25' width of this Hudson River tributary was frozen with snow-covered ice. We spotted river otter tracks out in the snow leading across a tongue of ice, disappearing down into a dark crevasse, into an open lead, and into the river. Red-breasted nuthatches were singing and coyote tracks in the snow lined the shore.

Newcomb, HRM 302: At one time or other, during the day, we managed to spot all three merganser species at Newcomb: red-breasted, common, and hooded. According to the Adirondack Visitors Information Center, the red-breasted mergansers winter and also nest in the area.

Ice Meadows on the equinox   by Tom Lake

Tahawus, HRM 307: From the trailhead at the Upper Works we hiked up the Calamity Brook trail. We had heard of the swath that tropical storm *Floyd* had cut across the Adirondacks but little could have prepared us for what we encountered. The Calamity Brook trail had forever been a path shaded by spruce and fir, on the way up into the High Peaks. Now the trail was a walk in the sunshine; the forest canopy was gone. Where we once had large tracts of forested land we now saw more open space than intact woodland. In all directions, deadfalls littered the landscape. To *Christopher Letts*, it looked as though "giants had been playing at jack straws." If something good could come from so much devastation, it might be that the blowdowns had created an abundance of edge habitat, a wildlife haven for much of the woodland animal community. In the snow along the trail we identified the tracks of pine marten, fisher, fox, and coyote. *Tom Lake* (See 9/17, Adirondack High Peaks.)

Town of Esopus, HRM 87: The first coltsfoot was blooming; in a few days it will be prevalent everywhere. *Fran Drakert, Bill Drakert*

3/23   Cornwall, HRM 57: It was the bottom of the ebb tide, just turning to flood, and the eagles of Cornwall Bay were feasting. We watched a pair of adults, side-by-side, perched in a tall cottonwood. They had each just finishing consuming a fish. We counted five more, all immature, on the tip-tops of snags out on the tideflats. Three of them were eating gizzard shad. *Fran Dunwell, Tom Lake*

Nyack, HRM 28: It was time once again to get ready for shad. Our forsythia was in bloom. a week early. *Bob Gabrielson*

Manhattan, HRM 5: In an average winter, New York City gets about 28" of snow. This winter New York City received only 15". *National Weather Service*

Kowawese
All the stuff I have seen
has made me change my way
of thinking about nature.
Nature is very important
and we see it only once.
Melissa Williams, New Windsor School, NY

Afterword

NY State Museum diorama of mastodont on the Hudson River at Kowawese

Printed by permission of the NYS Museum

In a year of many diverse natural phenomena--drought of historical proportions, an intense tropical storm, three new fish species, and many more bald eagles flying about--one event in particular changed the way many of us look at the Hudson River Valley. The Pleistocene elephant skeleton discovered at Hyde Park in September 1999, just a few miles from the river, gave the valley a time-depth that few of us had ever considered.

In a Volume VI poem, Brian Moriarty reminds us that the Hudson River Valley is "Exciting!" Brian captures the essence of why we step outside to see an eagle soar, a giant sturgeon leap, or to imagine an extinct elephant moving across a primeval landscape at the birth of the estuary. Exciting! And this sense of excitement has been around for a very long time.

We now fast-forward to **June 2000** to resume our search for the skeleton at Hyde Park. Paleontological Research Institution (PRI) site director *Warren Allmon* has returned to the kettle pond site for a week of investigation. While it had been established that the huge bones discovered in September 1999 were very old, the question still remained: To what extinct animal did they belong, and what could the discovery and analysis of the rest of the skeleton tell us about the Hudson River Valley of the late Pleistocene?

June 9, the kettle pond was drained to facilitate the search. The pond has three distinct layers: an 18" layer of dark organic peat, a 12" layer of lighter organic peat, and an 12" layer of marl (peat and clay mixture). These 3½ feet overlay the base of the pond, a fine blue-gray glacial clay. All week the weather alternated between torrential rain and wilting heat. Nothing more was discovered until the final day when Bridget Rigas caught a few tusk fragments as they slipped out of the backhoe's scoop. Discouraged at being unable to find the rest of the skeleton, PRI left the site.

June 30, for two days Vassar College Summer Scholars screened and collected floral and faunal material that had come from the base level of the pond. Carol Griggs, a Cornell University dendrochronology botanist, identified eleven tree species that grew in Hyde Park as much as 11,000 years ago. The evidence included fir and spruce cones, acorns, speckled alder catkins, hemlock charcoal, and willow leaf casts in clay. As we broke open some clods of clay and marl, we found insects that had been perfectly preserved for thousands of years. Bob Schmidt and John Chiment provided identification of a variety of species. PRI and Cornell paleontologists would use these data to reconstruct the Hyde Park ecosystem of the late Pleistocene.

August 20, PRI returned for two days of sampling—collecting sediments from the pond for analysis. The pond was pumped down but PRI had no expectations of finding any more of the skeleton.

August 21, at 6:45 PM, 15 minutes before PRI was going to leave the site for good, Elizabeth Humbert was taking her next-to-last core sample from the middle of the pond. She noticed something round and dark, barely protruding from the bottom of the pond. She knew immediately what it was: a sacrum, the skeletal point where the vertebral column meets the pelvis. The skeleton had been found. The marl was cleared away and before long a pelvis the size of a dining room table was exposed. But to what animal did it belong?

August 23, a 7½' long tusk, ribs, long bones, and vertebrae, were found in the marl layer near the pelvis. Still, nothing diagnostic of a specific animal had been discovered. Tusks are teeth, overgrown incisors, that lay down seasonal growth layers similar to tree rings. And, like trees, they can be dated. Dan Fisher, of the University of Michigan, estimated that this animal was a male aged 32-35 at the time of his death.

August 24, the animal's skull, the size of a refrigerator, was found. The molar teeth in the upper jaw confirmed our speculation. This was the skeleton of an **American mastodont**.

Mastodonts were proboscideans (they have a trunk) and are ancestral to modern elephants. Their lineage began in Africa with the oldest evidence coming from the Nile River Valley dating to thirty million years ago. They arrived in North America, probably across a glacial land bridge, around 14 million years ago. Adult mastodonts weighed 4-5 tons and were 8'-10' high at the shoulder. They were well adapted to the late Pleistocene Hudson Valley, a cool, boggy environment dominated by spruce and fir forests with some emerging hardwoods. Their teeth had evolved with cusps, similar to white-tailed deer, that were used to browse the spruce, fir, and hardwood understory. Pollen analysis has shown that in warm weather they also grazed on flowers, shrubs and emergent aquatic vegetation.

How old was this mastodont? David Burney and Guy Robinson, of Fordham University, had a tusk fragment analyzed. The radiocarbon (^{14}C) date determined that the tusk was about 11,500 years old.

September 27, the skeleton was taken to Ithaca for preservation. It will eventually be on display at the Paleontological Research Institution. An exact replica will be returned to Dutchess County.

How did this mastodont die? It is believed that mastodonts were highly social animals. The Lozier's kettle pond may have been a focus of daily life, a gathering place for socializing, drinking, feeding, and wallowing. Cornell's Vicki Chiment found evidence of mastodont dung in sediments at the base of the pond. Mastodont dung has a distinctive, pleasant, aroma and is characterized by twigs and branchlets, sheared on one end and mashed on the other. There are several hypotheses as to how this one died. It may have been sick or injured, became mired in the soft bottom, and drowned. There is a possibility that it may have been killed, or scavenged, by some of the first humans in the Hudson Valley. Mastodonts were one of a group of large mammals that went extinct at the end of the Pleistocene for reasons that may have ranged from human hunting to failure to adapt to a warming post ice-age environment. Careful analysis of these bones may provide a clue.

On **September 30**, the site was closed. For many of us it had been 392 days of mastodont mania, a once-in-a-lifetime opportunity. Finding this skeleton and working this excavation was like opening a time capsule from 12,000 years ago. For the scores of volunteers, it was like reading chapter one in the book of the Hudson Valley. The drama of this site was played out at a time when the mid-Hudson Valley was first becoming an estuary, the first Native Americans were entering the Northeast, and shortly before the time when these magnificent animals would become extinct. For a brief time we were all able to glimpse the Hudson Valley, Dutchess County, and Hyde Park, through a lens of great antiquity. We tossed a few shiny 2000 Lincoln pennies into the pit, turned off the pumps, and watched the pond fill back up. In a Volume VI poem, Melissa Williams reminds us that nature is very important, and how we see it only once. In this instance, we had the rare opportunity to see something that we had missed the first time.

Tom Lake
Editor

Appendix A. Common and Scientific Names of Flora and Fauna

Flora:
Bladder wrack *(Fucus vesiculosus)*
Balsam fir *(Abies balsamea)*
White spruce, *Picea glauca*
Red spruce *(Picea rubens)*
Pitch pine *(Pinus rigida)*
White pine *(Pinus strobus)*
Eastern hemlock *(Tsuga canadensis)*
Northern white cedar *(Thuja occidentalis)*
Yellow pondlily *(Nuphar advena)*
Snowdrops *(Anemone quinquefolia)*
Marsh marigold *(Caltha palustris)*
Hepatica *(Hepatica sp.)*
Rue anemone *(Thalictrum thalictroides)*
Japanese barberry *(Berberis thunbergii)*
Bloodroot *(Sanguinaria canadensis)*
Bladder campion *(Silene vulgaris)*
Rose-mallow *(Hibiscus moscheutos)*
Eastern sycamore *(Platanus occidentalis)*
American elm, *Ulmus americana*
American beech *(Fagus grandifolia)*
White oak *(Quercus alba)*
Scrub oak *(Quercus ilicifolia)*
Black oak *(Quercus nigricans)*
Red oak *(Quercus rubra)*
Speckled alder, *Alnus rugosa*
Sweet (black) birch *(Betula lenta)*
Appalachian sand-wort *(Minuartia glabra)*
Eastern cottonwood *(Populus deltoides)*
Quaking aspen *(Populus tremuloides)*
Black willow *(Salix nigra)*
Rock cress *(Arabis sp.)*
Dame's Rocket *(Hesperis matronalis)*
Mountain laurel (Kalmia latifolia)
Shadbush *(Amelanchier arborea)*
Beach plum *(Prunus maritima)*
Multiflora rose *(Rosa multiflora)*
Black raspberry *(Rubus occidentalis)*
Wineberry *(Rubus phoenicolasius)*
Bird's-foot trefoil *(Lotus corniculata)*
Red clover *(Trifolium pratense)*
Purple vetch *(Vicia americana)*
Wisteria *(Wisteria frutescens)*
Eurasian water milfoil *(Myriophyllum spicatum)*
Purple loosestrife *(Lythrum salicaria)*
Water chestnut *(Trapa natans)*
Flowering dogwood *(Cornus florida)*
Spurge *(Euphorbia sp.)*
Oriental bittersweet *(Celastrus orbiculatus)*
Wild grape *(Vitis sp.)*
Box elder *(Acer negundo)*

Red maple *(Acer rubrum)*
Sugar maple *(Acer saccharum)*
Poison ivy *(Toxicodendron radicans)*
Tree-of-heaven *(Ailanthus altissima)*
Spotted jewelweed *(Impatiens capensis)*
Black nightshade (Solanum ptycanthum)
Forsythia *(Forsythia sp.)*
Common lilac *(Syringa vulgaris)*
White bedstraw *(Galium mollugo)*
Japanese honeysuckle *(Lonicera japonica)*
Common yarrow *(Achillea millefolium)*
Alpine goldenrod *(Solidago multiradiata)*
Common dandelion *(Taraxacum officinale)*
Coltsfoot *(Tussilago farfara)*
Wild celery *(Vallisneria americana)*
Curly pondweed *(Potamogeton crispus)*
Clasping-leaved pondweed *(Potamogeton perfoliatus)*
Sharp-fruited rush *(Juncus acuminatus)*
Narrow-panicled rush *(Juncus brevicaudatus)*
Soft rush *(Juncus effusus)*
Grass-leaved rush *(Juncus marginatus)*
Woods-rush *(Juncus subcaudatus)*
Path rush *(Juncus tenuis)*
Three-square *(Scirpus americanus)*
Soft-stemmed bulrush *(Scirpus sp.)*
Common reed *(Phragmites australis)*
Wild rice *(Zizania aquatica)*
Arrow arum *(Peltandra virginica)*
Cattail *(Typha sp.)*
Pickerel-weed *(Pontederia cordata)*
Troutlily *(Erythronium americanum)*
Yellow flag *(Iris pseudacorus)*
Swamp pink *(Arethusa bulbosa)*
Pink ladyslipper *(Cypripedium acaule)*

Fauna
Mammals:
Little brown myotis *(Myotis lucifugus)*
Red bat *(Lasiurus borealis)*
Red squirrel *(Tamiasciurus hudsonicus)*
Gray squirrel *(Sciurus carolinensis)*
Red squirrel *(Tamiasciurus hudsonicus)*
Muskrat *(Ondatra zibethicus)*
Beaver *(Castor canadensis)*
Norway rat *(Rattus norvegicus)*
Eastern coyote *(Canis latrans)*
Red fox *(Vulpes vulpes)*
Black bear *(Ursus americanus)*
Raccoon *(Procyon lotor)*
Marten *(Martes americana)*

Fisher *(Martes pennanti)*
River otter *(Lutra canadensis)*
Bobcat *(Felis rufus)*
American mastodont *(Mammut americanum)*
Harbor porpoise *(Phocoena phocoena)*
Harbor seal *(Phoca vitulina)*
Giant bison *(Bison bison antiquus)*
White-tailed deer *(Odocoileus virginianus)*

Hominidae (464):
Contributors *(Homo sapiens)*

Birds:
Common loon *(Gavia immer)*
Horned grebe *(Podiceps auritus)*
Pied-billed grebe *(Podilymbus podiceps)*
Double-crested cormorant *(Phalacrocorax auritus)*
Great cormorant *(Phalacrocorax carbo)*
Great blue heron *(Ardea herodias)*
Green heron *(Butorides striatus)*
Great egret *(Casmerodius albus)*
Snowy egret *(Egretta thula)*
Black-crowned night heron *(Nycticorax nycticorax)*
Least bittern *(Ixobrychus exilis)*
Mute swan *(Cygnus olor)*
Tundra swan *(Olor columbianus)*
Canada goose *(Branta canadensis)*
Brant *(Branta bernicla)*
Snow goose *(Chen caerulescens)*
Mallard *(Anas platyrhynchos)*
Black duck *(Anas rubripes)*
Northern pintail *(Anas acuta)*
Green-winged teal *(Anas crecca)*
Blue-winged teal *(Anas discors)*
Wood duck *(Aix sponsa)*
White-winged scoter *(Melanitta deglandi)*
Ring-necked duck *(Aythya collaris)*
Canvasback *(Aythya valisineria)*
Greater scaup *(Aythya marila)*
Lesser scaup *(Aythya affinis)*
Common goldeneye *(Bucephala islandica)*
Bufflehead *(Bucephala albeola)*
Oldsquaw *(Clangula hyemalis)*
Ruddy duck *(Oxyura jamaicensis)*
Hooded merganser *(Lophodytes cucullatus)*
Common merganser *(Mergus merganser)*
Red-breasted merganser *(Mergus serrator)*
Turkey vulture *(Cathartes aura)*
Black vulture *(Coragyps atratus)*
Sharp-shinned hawk *(Accipiter striatus)*
Cooper's hawk *(Accipiter cooperii)*
Northern goshawk *(Accipiter gentilis)*
Red-tailed hawk *(Buteo jamaicensis)*
Rough-legged hawk *(Buteo lagopus)*

Red-shouldered hawk *(Buteo lineatus)*
Broad-winged hawk *(Buteo platypterus)*
Golden eagle *(Aquila chrysaetos)*
Bald eagle *(Haliaeetus leucocephalus)*
Northern harrier, Marsh hawk *(Circus cyaneus)*
Osprey *(Pandion haliaetus)*
Peregrine falcon *(Falco peregrinus)*
Merlin *(Falco columbarius)*
American kestrel *(Falco sparverius)*
Wild turkey *(Meleagris gallopavo)*
American coot *(Fulica americana)*
Killdeer *(Charadrius vociferus)*
Piping plover *(Charadrius melodus)*
Semipalmated plover *(Charadrius semipalmatus)*
Wilson's plover *(Charadrius wilsonia)*
Greater yellowlegs *(Tringa melanoleuca)*
Lesser yellowlegs *(Tringa flavipes)*
Upland sandpiper *(Bartramia longicauda)*
Pectoral sandpiper *(Calidris melanotos)*
Dunlin *(Calidris alpina)*
Solitary sandpiper *(Tringa solitaria)*
Spotted sandpiper *(Actitis macularia)*
Least sandpiper *(Calidris minutilla)*
Semipalmated sandpiper *(Calidris pusilla)*
Baird's sandpiper *(Calidris baidrii)*
Magnificent frigatebird *(Fregata magnificens)*
Herring gull *(Larus argentatus)*
Ring-billed gull *(Larus delawarensis)*
Iceland gull *(Larus glaucoides)*
Greater black-backed gull *(Larus marinus)*
Bonaparte's gull *(Larus philadelphia)*
Short-eared *(Asio flammeus)*
Long-eared *(Asio otus)*
Great-horned owl *(Bubo virginianus)*
Barred owl *(Strix varia)*
Barn owl *(Tyto alba)*
Saw-whet owl *(Aegolius acadicus)*
Eastern screech owl *(Otus asio)*
Mourning dove *(Zenaida macroura)*
Common ñighthawk *(Chordeiles minor)*
Chuck-will's-widow *(Caprimulgus carolinensis)*
Ruby-throated hummingbird *(Archilochus colubris)*
Belted kingfisher *(Megaceryle alcyon)*
Pileated woodpecker *(Dryocopus pileatus)*
Red-headed woodpecker *(Melanerpes erythrocephalus)*
Downy woodpecker *(Picoides pubescens)*
Eastern phoebe *(Sayornis phoebe)*
Eastern wood pewee *(Contopus virens)*
Willow flycatcher (Empidonax traillii)
Water pipit *(Anthus spinoletta)*
Tree swallow *(Iridoprocne bicolor)*
Chimney swift *(Chaetura pelagica)*
Blue jay *(Cyanocitta cristata)*

Black-capped chickadee *(Parus atricapillus)*
Tufted titmouse *(Parus bicolor)*
Fish crow *(Corvus ossifragus)*
Common crow *(Corvus brachyrhynchos)*
Common raven *(Corvus corax)*
Red-breasted nuthatch *(Sitta canadensis)*
Brown creeper *(Certhia familiaris)*
Marsh wren *(Cistothorus palutris)*
House wren *(Troglodytes aedon)*
Carolina wren *(Thryothorus ludovicianus)*
Winter wren *(Troglodytes troglodytes)*
Ruby-crowned kinglet *(Regulus calendula)*
Golden-crowned kinglet *(Regulus satrapa)*
Blue-gray gnatcatcher *(Polioptila caerulea)*
Northern mockingbird *(Mimus polyglottos)*
American robin *(Turdus migratorius)*
Eastern bluebird *(Sialia sialis)*
Veery *(Catharus fuscescens)*
Hermit thrush *(Catharus guttatus)*
Wood thrush *(Hylocichla mustelina)*
Cedar waxwing *(Bombycilla cedrorum)*
Northern shrike *(Lanius excubitor)*
Warbling vireo *(Vireo gilvus)*
Red-eyed vireo *(Vireo olivaceus)*
Bay-breasted warbler *(Dendroica castanea)*
Cerulean warbler *(Dendroica cerulea)*
Yellow-rumped warbler *(Dendroica coronata)*
Prairie warbler *(Dendroica discolor)*
Blackburian warbler *(Dendroica fusca)*
Magnolia warbler *(Dendroica magnolia)*
Palm warbler *(Dendroica palmarum)*
Chestnut-sided warbler *(Dendroica pensylvanica)*
Yellow warbler *(Dendroica petechia)*
Blackpoll warbler *(Dendroica striata)*
Cape May warbler *(Dendroica tigrini)*
Black-throated geeen warbler *(Dendroica virens)*
Worm-eating warbler *(Helmitheros vermivorus)*
American redstart *(Setophaga ruticilla)*
Tennessee warbler *((Vermivora peregrina)*
Hooded warbler *(Wilsonia citrina)*
Wilson's warbler *(Wilsonia pusilla)*
Common yellowthroat *(Geothlypis trichas)*
Yellow-breasted chat *(Icteria virens)*Louisiana
waterthrush *(Seiurus motacilla)*
Northern waterthrush *(Seiurus novenoracensis)*
Ovenbird *(Seiurus aurocapillus)*
Eastern meadowlark *(Sturnella magna)*
Red-winged blackbird *(Agelaius phoeniceus)*
European starling *(Sturnus vulgaris)*
Northern oriole *(Icterus galbula)*
Orchard oriole *(Icterus spurius)*
Common grackle *(Quiscalus quiscula)*
Brown-headed cowbird *(Molothrus ater)*
Bobolink *(Dolichonyx oryzivorus)*

Scarlet tanager *(Piranga olivacea)*
Lapland longspur *(Calcarius lapponicus)*
House finch *(Carpodacus mexicanus)*
Evening grosbeak *(Hesperiphona vespertina)*
Common redpoll *(Carduelis flammea)*
Hoary redpoll *(Carduelis hornemanni)*
Pine siskin *(Carduelis pinus)*
American goldfinch *(Carduelis tristis)*
Northern cardinal *(Cardinalis cardinalis)*
Red crossbill *(Loxia curvirostra)*
White-winged crossbill *(Loxia leucoptera)*
Dark-eyed junco *(Junco hyemalis)*
White-throated sparrow *(Zonotrichia albicollis)*
White-crowned sparrow *(Zonotrichia leucophrys)*
Song sparrow *(Charadrius melodus)*
Clay-colored sparrow *(Spizella pallida)*
Lincoln's sparrow *(Melospiza lincolni)*
Snow bunting *(Plectrophenax nivalis)*

Fish:
Shortnose sturgeon *(Acipenser brevirostrum)*
American eel *(Anguilla rostrata)*
Blueback herring *(Alosa aestivalis)*
Hickory shad *(Alosa mediocris)*
Alewife *(Alosa pseudoharengus)*
American shad *(Alosa sapidissima)*
Atlantic menhaden *(Brevoortia tyrannus)*
Atlantic herring *(Clupea harengus)*
Gizzard shad *(Dorosoma cepedianum)*
Bay anchovy *(Anchoa mitchilli)*
Goldfish *(Carassius auratus)*
Spotfin shiner *(Cyprinella spiloptera)*
Common carp *(Cyprinus carpio)*
Eastern silvery minnow, *(Hybognathus regius)*
Golden shiner *(Notemigonus crysoleucas)*
Emerald shiner *(Notropis atherinoides)*
Spottail shiner *(Notropis hudsonius)*
Bluntnose minnow *(Pimephales notatus)*
Rudd *(Scardinius erythrophthalmus)*
White sucker *(Catostomus commersoni)*
Pacu *(Piaractus brachypomus)*
White catfish *(Ameiurus catus)*
Brown bullhead *(Ameiurus nebulosus)*
Channel catfish *(Ictalurus punctatus)*
Brindled madtom *(Noturus miurus)*
Northern pike *(Esox lucius)*
Rainbow trout *(Oncorhynchus mykiss)*
Brown trout *(Salmo trutta)*
Brook trout *(Salvelinus fontinalis)*
Inshore lizardfish *(Synodus foetens)*
Atlantic tomcod *(Microgadus tomcod)*
Spotted hake *(Urophycis regia)*
Atlantic needlefish *(Strongylura marina)*
Banded killifish *(Fundulus diaphanus diaphanus)*

Mummichog *(Fundulus heteroclitus)*
Brook silverside *(Labidesthes sicculus)*
Atlantic silverside *(Menidia menidia)*
Lined seahorse *(Hippocampus erectus)*
Northern pipefish *(Syngnathus fuscus)*
Striped sea robin *(Prionotus evolans)*
White perch *(Morone americana)*
Striped bass *(Morone saxatilis)*
Gag *(Mycteroperca microlepis)*
Rock bass *(Ambloplites rupestris)*
Redbreast sunfish *(Lepomis auritis)*
Pumpkinseed *(Lepomis gibbosus)*
Bluegill *(Lepomis macrochirus)*
Smallmouth bass *(Micropterus dolomieu)*
Largemouth bass *(Micropterus salmoides)*
Black crappie *(Pomoxis nigromaculatus)*
Tessellated darter *(Etheostoma olmstedi)*
Yellow perch *(Perca flavescens)*
Logperch *(Percina peltata)*
Bluefish *(Pomatomus saltatrix)*
Crevalle jack *(Caranx hippos)*
Lookdown *(Selene vomer)*
Gray snapper *(Lutjanus griseus)*
Pinfish *(Lagodon rhomboides)*
Scup *(Stenotomus chrysops)*
Freshwater drum *(Aplodinotus grunniens)*
Weakfish *(Cynoscion regalis)*
Spot *(Leiostomus xanthurus)*
Tautog *(Tautoga onitis)*
Northern stargazer *(Astroscopus guttatus)*
Fat sleeper *(Dormitator maculatus)*
Naked goby *(Gobiosoma bosc)*
Highfin goby, *Gobionellus oceanicus*
Spanish mackerel *(Scomberomorus maculatus)*
Summer flounder *(Paralichthys dentatus)*
Windowpane *(Scophthalmus aquosus)*
Winter flounder *(Pleuronectes americanus)*
Hogchoker *(Trinectes maculatus)*
Scrawled cowfish, *Acanthostracion quadricornis*
Northern puffer *(Sphoeroides maculatus)*

Amphibians:
Red-spotted newt *(Notophthalmus viridescens viridescens)*
American toad *(Bufo americanus)*
Spring peeper *(Pseudacris crucifer)*
Northern cricket frog *(Acris crepitans crepitans)*
Bullfrog *(Rana catesbeiana)*
Green frog *(Rana clamitans clamitans)*

Reptiles:
Snapping turtle *(Chelydra serpentina)*
Wood turtle *(Clemmys insculpta)*

Northern diamondback terrapin *(Malaclemys terrapin terrapin)*
Black rat snake *(Elaphe obsoleta obsoleta)*
Northern water snake *(Nerodia sipedon sipedon)*

Crustacea:
Rock crab *(Cancer irroratus)*
Atlantic blue crab *(Callinectes sapidus)*
Lady crab *(Ovalipes ocellatus)*
White-fingered mud crab *(Rhithropanopeus harrisii)*
Japanese green crab *(Hemigrapsus sanguineus)*
River crayfish *(Orconectes limosus)*
Bay barnacle *(Balanus improvisus)*
Red-jointed fiddler crab *(Uca minax)*
Sand shrimp *(Crangon septemspinosa)*
Shore shrimp, Grass shrimp *(Palaemonetes pugio)*

Mollusca:
Jingle shell *(Amonia simplex)*
Zebra mussel *(Dreissena polymorpha)*
Pisidium adamsi
Wedge rangia *(Rangia cuneata)*
Common oyster *(Crassostrea virginica)*
Cowrie shells *(Cypraea* sp.)
Balthic macoma *(Macoma balthica)*
Soft-shelled clams *(Mya arenaria)*
Ribbed mussels *(Modiolus demissus)*
Valvata lewisi
Valvata tricarinata
Fossaria decampi
Gyraulus parvus
Helisoma anceps, [form "striata"]

Insecta:
Periodical cicada (Magicicada)
Katydid *(Pterophylla* sp.)
Hemlock woolly adelgid (Adelges tsugae)
Springtail (Collembola)
Pipevine swallowtail *(Battus philenor)*
Monarch butterfly *(Danaus plexippus)*
Mourning cloak butterfly *(Nymphalis antiopa)*
Tiger swallowtail butterfly *(Papilio glaucus)*
Pearl crescent *(Phyciodes tharos)*
Cloudless sulphur butterfly *(Phoebis sennae)*
Spring azure *(Celastrina argiolus)*
Polyphemus silkworm moth *(Antheraea polyphemus)*

Ctenophora:
Beroe's comb jelly *(Beroe cucumis)*

Semeaostomeae:
Moon jelly *(Aurelia aurita)*

Appendix B: Scientific Advisory Committee

Dr. Stuart Findlay
Aquatic Ecologist
Institute of Ecosystem Studies

Dr. Erik Kiviat
Science Director
Hudsonia, Ltd.

Dr. Robert Schmidt
Professor
Simon's Rock of Bard College

Appendix C: References and Literature Cited

Boyle, Robert H.
> 1969 *The Hudson River, a Natural and Unnatural History.* W.W. Norton & Company, Inc. NY.

Dunne, Pete, David Sibley, and Clay Sutton
> 1988 *Hawks in Flight.* Houghton Mifflin Company, Boston, MA.

Gosner, Kenneth L.
> 1971 *Guide to Identification of Marine and Estuarine Invertebrates.* John Wiley & Sons, NY.

King, A., *et al.*
> 1999 *A Walk Through Time,* edited by Eileen Fontanella, and Andrea Letizia. A Hendrick Hudson High School Publication, Montrose, NY.

Lake, Thomas R., & Bethia Waterman
> 1996 *Hudson River Almanac,* Vol.I 1994-1995. New York State Department of Environmental Conservation, Albany, NY.

> 1996 *Hudson River Almanac,* Vol.II 1995-1996. Purple Mountain Press, Fleischmanns, NY.

> 1997 *Hudson River Almanac,* Vol.III 1996-1997. Purple Mountain Press, Fleischmanns, NY.

> 1998 *Hudson River Almanac,* Vol.IV 1997-1998. Purple Mountain Press, Fleischmanns, NY.

> 1999 *Hudson River Almanac,* Vol.V 1998-1999. Purple Mountain Press, Fleischmanns, NY.

Nicodema, C., *et al.*
> 1999 *The Hudson River Book: A Book of Poetry by P.R.M.S. 6th Grade Students.* Pearl River Middle School, Pearl River, NY.

Oliver, Barbara, Donna Sutton, Debbie Bacon, and Sharon Best
> 2000 *River of Words: Poems Written by the Sixth Grade New Windsor School, January 2000.* New Windsor Elementary School, New Windsor, NY.

Peterson, Roger Tory
> 1980 *A Field Guide to Birds.* Houghton Mifflin Company, Boston, MA.

Smith, C. Lavett
> 1985 *The Inland Fishes of New York State.* New York State Department of Environmental Conservation. Albany, NY.

Walls, Jerry G.
> 1975 *Fishes of the Northern Gulf of Mexico.* T.F.H. Publications, Inc. Ltd. Neptune City, NJ.

Appendix D. List of Contributors: 464

Rie Akazawa
Meg Aldrich
Jennifer Alexander
Ruth Allen
Ted Allen
Warren Allmon
Christie Alvarez
Hollie Amsler
Ned Ames
Edward Anacker
Rich Anderson
Russell Anderson
Helena Andreyko
Jacklin Aronchick
Martin Aronchick
Russel Aronchick
John Askildsen
William Atkins
Frank Auriemna
Jason Baldwin
Rick Banducci
Mike Bannan
Brenda Bates
Joan Bates
Margaret Bates
Anniker Beard
Christopher Beard
Karl Beard
Nancy Beard
Jim Beemer
Denise Beirne
Robin Bell
Eric Bender
Dery Bennett
Bill Berks
Larry Bickford
Larry Biegel
Jane Byers Bierhorst
John Bierhorst
Amy Bilbao
Laura Bilbao
Lorenzo Bilbao
Zachery Bilbao
Bev Bischoff
Betsy Blair
Andy Blanchette
Glenn Blank
Doug Bloom
Michael Bochnik
Bonnie Bogumil
Sandy Bonardi

Aime Bourdon
Gretchen Bowman
Marguerite Bowman
Chris Bowser
Robert H. Boyle
Sue Bride
Mary Brockway
Larry Brown
B. Buchanan
Dick Buckey
Rich Buckey Jr.
Mark Burch
Sandra Bureau
David Burney
Debbie Bush
Gary Bush
Bobbi Buske
Ted Caldwell
Kimberly Cantone
Jim Capossela
Jim Carey
Pam Carlsen
Jim Casey
Marissa Chabon
Andy Chadwick
Elieen Chadwick
Evan Chadwick
Patrick Chadwick
Mary Chalaney
Judy Chamberlain
Anna Chazkel
John Chiment
Vicki Chiment
Benjamin Chrobot
Felice Ciccione
Sue Clifford
Jonathan Cole
Gale Collins
Christopher Colume
Maynard Colume
Rosemary Compton
Brian Connolly
David Conover
John Conroy
Pat Coren
Betty Corey
Michael Corey
Sue Corey
Amanda Cosman
Lauren Dalrymple
A. Danforth

Robert Daniels
David Darr
Scott Davis
Liz DeAngelis
Brendan Delaney
Lou Del Santo
Brian Derr
Amanda deSilva
Robert deVilleneuve
Wayne Deyo
Danielle Diamaiolo
Joseph Diamond
Antonio Diaz
Joe Diebboll
Brian DiGirolamo
George Doere
Ann Marie Dolan
Phil Dominicio
Casey Donohue
Nicole Donovan
Amelia Dosio
Roger Downs
Bill Drakert
Fran Drakert
Cathy Drew
Jean Drusik
Joe Dunn
Fran Dunwell
Kim Durham
Eric Eckley
Lawson Edgar
Jim Elkin
Fred Ellman
Lloyd Ellman
Nancy Engel
Connie Eristoff
Anne P. Sidamon-
    Eristoff
Cheryl Esper
John Esper
Melissa Everett
Lynn Falbella
Kathryn Ferrara
Pat Festa
Johnathan Figueroa
Stuart Findlay
Dan Fisher
Murray Fisher
Tom Fitzpatrick
Mike Flaherty
Asia Flemister

Dorothy Fleury
Maggie Fontanella
Alfred Francese
Lydia Francese
Vincent Francese
Matt Frohman
Robert Funk
Bob Gabrielson
Joan Gabrielson
Robert Gabrielson Jr.
Melissa Gallo
Gino Garner
Ron Gelardi
Regina Gelman
Alon Gordon
Dick Grace
Matt Graff
Evelyn Greene
Carrie Grey
Carol Griggs
Brad Hake
Ellen Hake
Henrietta Hake
Tom Hake
Harry Hall
Wayne Hall
Barbara Hargraves
Michael Hargraves
Earl Harkins
Rachel Harris
Kathy Hattala
Gene Heinemeyer
Bill Herguth
Carolyn Herguth
Charles Herman
Kristy Herman
Jason Hernandez
Jon Herzog
Clay Hiles
George Hockman
Gregg Hogancamp
Nordica Holochuck
Anne Horst
Henry Hudson
Elizabeth Humbert
Lynn Hunt
Tom Hurst
Steffen Hyder
Ron Ingold
Jesse Jaycox
Paul Jebb

Tim Jones
Ann Joseph
Susan Joseph
Andy Kahnle
Bob Kakerbeck
David Karrman
Dick Kearns
Barry Keegan
Chuck Keene
Walt Keller
Frank Kendrick
Jim Kennedy
Robert Kennedy Jr.
Jenette Kerr
Steve Kessler
Bob Keyes
Abby King
Amy King
David King
Harold King
Lou Kingsley
Erik Kiviat
Esther Kiviat
John Klonowski
Chris Kocher
Wayne Kocher
Bryan Kress
Paul Krohn
Dick Lahey
Christopher Lake
Margaret Lake
Phyllis Lake
Susanne Lake
Tom Lake
Carolyn Lavallee
Steve Lawrence
Fred LeBrun
Edward Lenik
Christopher Letts
Nancy Letts
Karin Limburg
Eric Lind
Dave Lindemann
Christopher Linder
Buddy Long
Stephanie Roberg-
    Lopez
Cathy Lozier
Larry Lozier
Sheryl Lozier
Tom Lozier
Doug Maass
Sean Madden
Cesare Manfredi

Jennifer March
Carl Marchese
Gene Martin
Fran Martino
Karen Martis
Anton Masterovoy
Sofiya Masterovoy
Stephanie Matteson
Connie Mayer
Kathy McCarthy
Dave McCutcheon
Lori McKean
Kim McKown
Allan Michelin
Barbara Michelin
Gail Mihocko
Bob Miller
Dick Miller
Megan Molique
Rick Molique
Denis Moran
Lucy Moran
Marc Moran
Sadie Moran
Tom Moran
Brian Moriarity
Charles Morse
Vera Morse
John Moyle
Bill Murray
Marianne Murray
John Mylod
Everett Nack
Jennifer Naegeli
Leon Najman
Davis Natzle
Lia Natzle
Dick Nelson
Pete Nester
Will Nixon
Peter Nye
Ellen O'Connell
Joseph O'Connell
John O'Connor
Craig O'Donnell
Debbie O'Donnell
Ruth Olbert
Kevin Oldenberg
Yelena Olevskaia
Barbara Oliver
Susan Olsen
Edwin Ortega
Darren O'Sullivan
Kristen O'Toole

Elizabeth Pacahuala
Miguel Padilla
Alex Papo
Laura Papo
Earl Pardini
Richard E. Park
Frank Parslow Jr.
George E. Pataki
April Paupst
Craig Paupst
Robert Pearson Jr.
Nick Peck
Tom Perry
Kathleen Peterson
Diane Picciano
Philip Picciano
Ron Pierce
Sherry Piesco
Mark Plummer
Jayson Porrod
Ian Powell
Jon Powell
Chris Pray
James Prester
Sharonrose Pullian
Chip Putnam
Bob Rancan
Janet Rancan
Steve Raphael
Ian Raywid
Phil Redo
Doug Reed
Clive Richards
Bridget Rigas
Guy Robinson
Dee Rod
Doug Rod
Lyn Roessler
Amanda Rogers
David Rokoszynski
Andrew Rose
Estelle Rosen
Sidney Rosen
David Rosenfeld
Carolyn Rounds
Phil Rounds
Steve Ruff
Stephanie Rundle
Maciej Samela
Christopher Scarcella
Jim Scarcella
John Scardefield
Stacy Scardefield
Steven Scardefield

Rebecca Schavrien
Amy Scher
Alec Schmidt
Kathy Schmidt
Robert Schmidt
Smokey Schools
Tom Schroeder
Mrs. Gustave Schulz
Rev. Gustave Schulz
Kimberly Schwab
Ricardo Sealy
Pete Seeger
Carol Setchko
Lisa Seymour
Stephen Seymour
Jean Shaw
Ken Shaw
Joan Sheppard
Jim Sherpa
Elijah Shiffer
Isis Shiffer
Michael Shiffer
Evan Shornstein
Amy Silberkleit
John B. Skiba
Nancy Slowik
C. Lavett Smith
Danielle Smith
Doug Smith
Howard Smith
Oren Smith
Ross Smith
Steve Smith
Jim Sotis
Sandy Sprague
Jim Spohr
Andra Sramek
Ron Stanford
Margaret Stanne
Steve Stanne
Paul Stanton
Nancy Steinberg
Gretchen Stevens
Ed Stinson
Ward Stone
George Story
John Stowell
Gerry Straight
Agnes Strassner
David Strayer
Rick Sullivan
Dan Sunderlin
Dennis Suszkowski
Donna Sutton

Appendix E: Catch-Per-Unit-of-Effort (CPUE): 1999

Relative fish and crustacean abundance expressed as number of animals per meter of linear distance seined.
YOY = young of the year

6/24   North Germantown, HRM 109:
55'x6'seine; water 76 °F; salinity 0.0 ppt

spottail shiner	0.81	YOY
blueback herring	0.54	YOY
striped bass	0.49	YOY
banded killifish	0.12	
white perch	0.12	YOY
banded killifish	0.06	YOY
tessellated darter	0.01	YOY

Nutten Hook, HRM 124: *55'x6'seine; water 76 °F;*
salinity 0.0 ppt

blueback herring	5.07	YOY
spottail shiner	4.93	YOY
striped bass	2.93	YOY
white perch	0.75	YOY
banded killifish	0.72	
alewife	0.36	YOY
banded killifish	0.36	YOY
tessellated darter	0.06	YOY
spottail shiner	0.03	
white perch	0.03	

7/12   North Germantown, HRM 109:
15'x6'seine; water 78 °F; salinity 0.0 ppt

striped bass	7.38	YOY
alewife	6.01	YOY
Atlantic menhaden	4.92	YOY
blueback herring	4.10	YOY
spottail shiner	1.31	YOY
banded killifish	1.18	
white perch	0.98	YOY
emerald shiner	0.66	

banded killifish	0.60	YOY
redbreast sunfish	0.38	
smallmouth bass	0.11	YOY

Nutten Hook, HRM 124: *15'x6'seine; water 78 °F;*
salinity 0.0 ppt

alewife	3.17	YOY
striped bass	3.06	YOY
blueback herring	2.40	YOY
Atlantic menhaden	0.98	YOY
white perch	0.77	YOY
spottail shiner	0.61	YOY
emerald shiner	0.18	YOY
tessellated darter	0.13	YOY
Atlantic blue crab	0.07	
American eel	0.02	

Mohawk River, Waterford, HRM 158:
15'x6'seine; water 77 °F; salinity 0.0 ppt

blueback herring	2.84	YOY
spotfin shiner	1.71	YOY
spottail shiner	0.48	YOY
bluntnose minnow	0.48	YOY
brook silverside	0.48	YOY
emerald shiner	0.40	YOY
smallmouth bass	0.31	YOY
yellow perch	0.28	YOY
pumpkinseed sunfish	0.26	
rock bass	0.24	YOY
logperch	0.20	
redbreast sunfish	0.13	
tessellated darter	0.13	YOY
yellow perch	0.11	

largemouth bass	0.09	YOY
largemouth bass	0.07	

7/22 North Germantown, HRM 109:
85'x4'seine; water 79 °F; salinity 0.0 ppt

American shad	0.76	YOY
striped bass	0.51	YOY
blueback herring	0.31	YOY
spottail shiner	0.16	YOY
alewife	0.10	YOY
banded killifish	0.07	YOY
banded killifish	0.06	
white perch	0.05	YOY
redbreast sunfish	0.01	YOY
smallmouth bass	0.01	YOY
largemouth bass	0.01	YOY

Nutten Hook, HRM 124: *15'x6'seine; water 79 °F; salinity 0.0 ppt*

American shad	1.46	YOY
striped bass	0.56	YOY
spottail shiner	0.42	YOY
alewife	0.26	YOY
white perch	0.07	YOY
tessellated darter	0.02	YOY
blueback herring	0.01	YOY

Mohawk River, Waterford, HRM 158:
15'x6'seine; water 78 °F; salinity 0.0 ppt

blueback herring	0.90	YOY
brook silverside	0.61	YOY
spotfin shiner	0.26	YOY
spottail shiner	0.13	YOY
emerald shiner	0.09	YOY
bluntnose minnow	0.08	YOY
smallmouth bass	0.08	YOY
logperch	0.08	
largemouth bass	0.06	YOY
rock bass	0.05	YOY
pumpkinseed sunfish	0.05	
redbreast sunfish	0.04	
tessellated darter	0.04	YOY
largemouth bass	0.01	
yellow perch	0.01	
yellow perch	0.01	YOY

8/12 North Germantown, HRM 109:
20'x6'seine; water 78 °F; salinity 0.0 ppt

alewife	0.46	YOY
striped bass	0.37	YOY
American shad	0.30	YOY
blueback herring	0.25	YOY
spottail shiner	0.23	YOY
banded killifish	0.10	YOY

banded killifish	0.07	
white perch	0.05	YOY
bluegill	0.04	YOY
smallmouth bass	0.03	YOY
largemouth bass	0.03	YOY
redbreast sunfish	0.02	
eastern silvery minnow	0.01	

Nutten Hook, HRM 124: *20'x6'seine; water 78 °F; salinity 0.0 ppt*

blueback herring	2.19	YOY
striped bass	0.88	YOY
spottail shiner	0.77	YOY
alewife	0.55	YOY
American shad	0.40	YOY
white perch	0.38	YOY
tessellated darter	0.09	YOY

Mohawk River, Waterford, HRM 158:
20'x6'seine; water 78 °F; salinity 0.0 ppt

brook silverside	0.58	YOY
spotfin shiner	0.43	YOY
blueback herring	0.36	YOY
spottail shiner	0.21	YOY
bluntnose minnow	0.12	YOY
smallmouth bass	0.09	YOY
pumpkinseed sunfish	0.08	
bluntnose minnow	0.07	
largemouth bass	0.07	YOY
redbreast sunfish	0.05	
bluegill	0.05	
emerald shiner	0.03	YOY
rock bass	0.03	YOY
tessellated darter	0.03	YOY
logperch	0.03	
largemouth bass	0.01	
yellow perch	0.01	
yellow perch	0.01	YOY

8/28 Croton Point, HRM 35: *85'x4'seine; water 83 °F; salinity 8.5 ppt*

American shad	1.04	YOY
Atlantic silverside	0.46	YOY
shore shrimp	0.42	
white perch	0.41	YOY
striped bass	0.31	YOY
Atlantic blue crab	0.25	
northern pipefish	0.17	YOY
bluefish	0.14	YOY
northern pipefish	0.08	
spot	0.08	YOY

9/11 Nutten Hook, HRM 124: *30'x6'seine; water 75 °F; salinity 0.0 ppt*

blueback herring	3.28	YOY
spottail shiner	0.72	YOY
alewife	0.52	YOY
white perch	0.26	YOY
Atlantic menhaden	0.20	YOY
striped bass	0.13	YOY
tessellated darter	0.03	YOY

9/14 Nyack Beach State Park, HRM 31: *50'x8'seine; water 75 °F; salinity 9.5 ppt*

Atlantic silverside	3.93	YOY
Atlantic blue crab	2.46	YOY
striped bass	1.02	YOY
Atlantic silverside	0.72	
white perch	0.46	YOY
bluefish	0.20	YOY
northern pipefish	0.13	YOY
shore shrimp	0.13	
Atlantic menhaden	0.10	YOY
northern pipefish	0.07	
sand shrimp	0.07	
spot	0.03	YOY

9/23 Kowawese, HRM 59: *85'x4'seine; water 71 °F; salinity < 2.0 ppt*

alewife	0.46	YOY
American shad	0.31	YOY
striped bass	0.19	YOY
white perch	0.04	YOY
Atlantic blue crab	0.04	YOY
gizzard shad	0.02	YOY
pumpkinseed	0.02	YOY
largemouth bass	0.02	YOY

9/24 North Germantown, HRM 109: *30'x6'seine; water 63 °F; salinity 0.0 ppt*

American shad	0.45	YOY
alewife	0.31	YOY
striped bass	0.25	YOY
redbreast sunfish	0.21	YOY
spottail shiner	0.20	YOY
banded killifish	0.05	
white perch	0.05	YOY
redbreast sunfish	0.04	
blueback herring	0.01	YOY

9/26 Croton Point, HRM 35: *200'x6'seine; water 68 °F; salinity 2.0 ppt*

Atlantic menhaden	3.83	YOY
white perch	0.82	
striped bass	0.82	YOY
bluefish	0.55	YOY

Atlantic blue crab	0.15	
white sucker	0.01	
weakfish	0.01	YOY

10/11 Kowawese, HRM 59: *85'x4'seine; water 60 °F; salinity < 2.0 ppt*

blueback herring	1.02	YOY
white perch	0.82	YOY
striped bass	0.82	YOY
alewife	0.62	YOY
American shad	0.45	YOY
spottail shiner	0.21	
Atlantic menhaden	0.10	YOU
gizzard shad	0.03	

10/12 North Germantown, HRM 109: *30'x6'seine; water 57 °F; salinity 0.0 ppt*

spottail shiner	0.22	YOY
alewife	0.21	YOY
American shad	0.19	YOU
striped bass	0.10	YOY
white perch	0.08	YOY
blueback herring	0.07	YOY
redbreast sunfish	0.04	YOY
banded killifish	0.03	YOY
Atlantic menhaden	0.02	YOY
golden shiner	0.01	YOY
emerald shiner	0.01	
smallmouth bass	0.01	YOY

10/14 Kowawese, HRM 59: *85'x4'seine; water 58 °F; salinity < 2.0 ppt*

blueback herring	0.88	YOY
striped bass	0.39	YOY
American shad	0.27	YOY
alewife	0.21	YOY
white perch	0.17	YOY
spottail shiner	0.07	YOY
golden shiner	0.06	YOY
tessellated darter	0.03	YOY
bay barnacle		

10/20 Croton Point, HRM 35: *20'x6'seine; water 58 °F; salinity 2.2 ppt*

blueback herring	3.44	YOY
American shad	0.98	YOY
alewife	0.49	YOY

10/26 Kowawese, HRM 59: *55'x6'seine; water 57 °F; salinity < 2.0 ppt*

blueback herring	0.76	YOY
spottail shiner	0.36	YOY
American shad	0.31	YOY
alewife	0.25	YOY

| white perch | 0.06 | YOY |
| striped bass | 0.01 | YOY |

10/29   Englewood, NJ, HRM 13.5: *50'x8'seine; water 55 °F; salinity 11.7 ppt*

Atlantic blue crab	0.97	YOY
American shad	0.41	YOY
striped bass	0.37	YOY
Atlantic silverside	0.29	
sand shrimp	0.15	
bay anchovy	0.12	YOY
shore shrimp	0.06	
gizzard shad	0.02	
white perch	0.02	

10/30   Englewood, NJ, HRM 13.5: *50'x8'seine; water 55 °F; salinity 12.1 ppt*

striped bass	0.68	YOY
Atlantic blue crab	0.54	YOY
American shad	0.48	YOY
Atlantic silverside	0.42	YOY
winter flounder	0.14	
sand shrimp	0.06	
white perch	0.02	
cowrie shell		
common oyster		

10/31   Englewood, NJ, HRM 13.5: *50'x8'seine; water 54 °F; salinity 12.2 ppt*

Atlantic blue crab	0.77	YOY
striped bass	0.39	YOY
American shad	0.39	YOY
white perch	0.02	
crevalle jack	0.02	

11/5   Englewood, NJ, HRM 13.5: *50'x8'seine; water 54 °F; salinity 11.5 ppt*

striped bass	0.39	YOY
Atlantic silverside	0.33	YOY
Atlantic blue crab	0.19	YOY
American shad	0.02	YOY
blueback herring	0.02	YOY
cowrie shell		

Appendix F: Hudson River Fish Fauna Check List

Lampreys
1. lamprey, silver
2. lamprey, American brook
3. lamprey, sea

Requiem sharks
4. shark (bull shark?)

Dogfish sharks
5. dogfish, smooth

Houndsharks
6. dogfish, spiny

Skates
7. skate, little
8. skate, barndoor

Sturgeons
9. sturgeon, shortnose
10. sturgeon, Atlantic

Gars
11. gar, longnose

Bowfins
12. bowfin

Tarpons
13. ladyfish

Bonefishes
14. bonefish

Freshwater eels
15. eel, American

Snake eels
16. worm eel, speckled

Conger eels
17. eel, conger

Herrings
18. herring, blueback
19. shad, hickory
20. alewife
21. shad, American
22. menhaden, Atlantic
23. herring, Atlantic
24. shad, gizzard
25. herring, round

Anchovies
26. anchovy, striped
27. anchovy, bay

Minnows
28. stoneroller, central
29. goldfish
30. dace, redside
31. chub, lake
32. carp, grass
33. shiner, satinfin
34. shiner, spotfin

35. carp, common
    koi, mirror carp *(var.)*
36. minnow, cutlips
37. minnow, brassy
38. minnow, eastern silvery
39. shiner, bridle
40. shiner, common
41. dace, pearl
42. chub, hornyhead
43. shiner, golden
44. shiner, comely
45. shiner, emerald
46. shiner, blackchin
47. shiner, blacknose
48. shiner, spottail
49. shiner, sand
50. shiner, rosyface
51. dace, northern redbelly
52. dace, finescale
53. minnow, bluntnose
54. minnow, fathead
55. dace, eastern blacknose
56. dace, longnose
57. bitterling
58. rudd
59. chub, creek
60. fallfish

Suckers
61. sucker, longnose
62. sucker, white
63. chubsucker, creek
64. hog sucker, northern
65. redhorse, shorthead

Characins
66. pacu

Catfishes
67. catfish, white
68. bullhead, yellow
69. bullhead, brown
70. catfish, channel
71. stonecat
72. madtom, tadpole
73. madtom, margined
74. madtom, brindled

Pikes
75. pickerel, redfin
76. pike, northern
    muskellunge, tiger
77. pickerel, chain

Mudminnows
78. mudminnow, central
79. mudminnow, eastern

Smelts
80. smelt, rainbow

Trouts
81. herring, lake *(cisco)*
82. whitefish, lake
83. trout, rainbow
84. kokanee *(sockeye)*
85. salmon, chinook
86. whitefish, round
87. salmon, Atlantic
88. trout, brown
89. trout, brook
90. trout, lake

Lizardfishes
91. lizardfish, inshore

Trout-perches
92. trout-perch

Codfishes
93. rockling, fourbeard
94. cod, Atlantic
95. hake, silver *(whiting)*
96. tomcod, Atlantic
97. pollock
98. hake, red *(ling)*
99. hake, spotted
100. hake, white

Cusk-eels
101. cusk-eel, striped

Toadfishes
102. toadfish, oyster

Goosefishes
103. goosefish *(anglerfish)*
9
Needlefishes
104. needlefish, Atlantic
105. houndfish

Killifishes
106. minnow, sheepshead
107. killifish, eastern banded
108. mummichog
109. killifish, spotfin
110. killifish, striped

Livebearers
111. mosquitofish, western

Silversides
112. silverside, brook
113. silverside, rough
114. silverside, inland
115. silverside, Atlantic

Sticklebacks
116. stickleback, fourspine
117. stickleback, brook
118. stickleback, threespine
119. stickleback, ninespine

Cornetfishes
120. cornetfish, bluespotted

Pipefishes
121. seahorse, lined
122. pipefish, northern

Flying gurnards
123. gurnard, flying

Sea robins
124. sea robin, northern
125. sea robin, striped

Sculpins
126. sculpin, slimy
127. sea raven
128. grubby
129. sculpin, longhorn

Snailfishes
130. lumpfish
131. seasnail, Atlantic

River basses
132. perch, white
133. bass, white
134. bass, striped

Sea basses
135. sea bass, black
136. gag *(grouper)*

Sunfishes
137. bass, rock
138. sunfish, bluespotted
139. sunfish, banded
140. sunfish, redbreast
141. sunfish, green

142. pumpkinseed
143. warmouth
144. bluegill
145. bass, smallmouth
146. bass, largemouth
147. crappie, white
148. crappie, black

Perches
149. darter, greenside
150. darter, fantail
151. darter, tessellated
152. perch, yellow
153. logperch
154. darter, shield
155. walleye

Bigeyes
156. bigeye, short

Bluefishes
157. bluefish

Cobias
158. cobia

Remoras
159. sharksucker

Jacks
160. jack, crevalle
161. moonfish, Atlantic
162. lookdown
163. permit

Snappers
164 . snapper, gray *(mangrove)*

Mojarras
165. mojarra, spotfin

Grunts
166. pigfish

Porgies
167. pinfish
168. scup *(porgy)*

Drums
169. drum, freshwater
170. perch, silver
171. weakfish
172. spot *(Lafayette)*
173. kingfish, northern

174. croaker, Atlantic

Butterflyfishes
175. butterflyfish, foureye
176. butterflyfish, spotfin

Mullets
177. mullet, striped
178. mullet, white

Barracudas
179. sennet, northern
180. guaguanche

Wrasses
181. tautog *(blackfish)*
182. cunner *(bergall, chogy)*

Gunnels
183. gunnel, rock

Stargazers
184. stargazer, northern

Combtooth blennies
185. blenny, feather
186. blenny, freckled

Sand lances
187. sand lance, American

Sleepers
188. sleeper, fat

Gobies
189. highfin goby
190. goby, naked
191. goby, seaboard

Snake mackerels
192. cutlassfish, Atlantic

Mackerels
193. mackerel, Atlantic
194. mackerel, Spanish

Butterfish
195. butterfish

Lefteyed flounders
196. flounder, Gulf Stream
197. flounder, smallmouth
198. flounder, summer *(fluke)*
199. flounder, fourspot

200. windowpane

Righteyed flounders
201. flounder, winter
202. flounder, yellowtail

Soles
203. tonguefish, northern
204. hogchoker

Leatherjackets
205. filefish, orange
206. filefish, planehead

Boxfishes
207. cowfish, scrawled

Puffers
208. burrfish, striped
209. puffer, smooth
210. puffer, northern

Diversity:

Classes	4
Orders	26
Families	73
Genera	149
Species	210

Appendix G. Observation Form

Hudson River Estuary Program
New York State Department of Environmental Conservation
21 South Putt Corners Road
New Paltz, NY 12561-1696
(845) 256-3016   FAX (845) 255-3649

John P. Cahill
Commissioner

Hudson River Almanac Observation Form

1. Date—Time (When):_____

2. Name (Who): _____   3. Phone: (___)_____

4. Address: _____

5. Observation locality, e.g., village, town, tributary, Hudson River mile (Where):

_____

_____

6. Describe observation, e.g., species, behavior, event (What):_____

_____

_____

_____

7. Significant environmental conditions, e.g., weather, wind, storm, water quality:

_____

8. Comments:_____

_____

Please return to:
Tom Lake
7 Steinhaus Lane
Wappinger Falls, NY 12590-3927
phone and fax: 845-297-8935; email: trlake7@aol.com

HUDSON RIVER WATERSHED

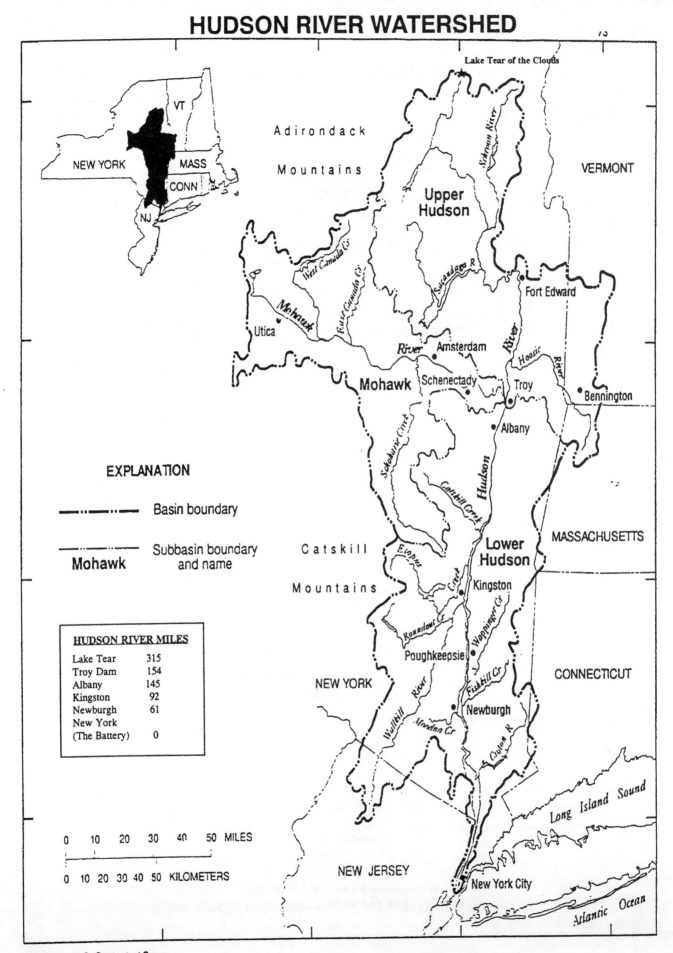

EXPLANATION

—··—··— Basin boundary

—·—·—·— Subbasin boundary
and name

Mohawk

HUDSON RIVER MILES	
Lake Tear	315
Troy Dam	154
Albany	145
Kingston	92
Newburgh	61
New York (The Battery)	0

0 10 20 30 40 50 MILES

0 10 20 30 40 50 KILOMETERS

Base from U.S. Geological Survey

Appendix I: Index of Flora, Fauna, and Hudson River Locations

Purple Mountain Press is a publishing company committed to producing the best original books of regional interest as well as bringing back into print significant older works. For a free catalog of more than 300 books about New York State, write: Purple Mountain Press, Ltd., PO Box 309, Fleischmanns, NY 12430, or call: 845-254-4062, or fax: 845-254-4476.